This true, inspiring story is dedicated to the nurses, doctors, volunteers, and administration of Phoenix Children's Hospital in Phoenix, Arizona; a place not only of medicine, but also one of hope, inspiration, compassion, and enlightenment.

For all the prayers, good thoughts, and unyielding support through the darkest days in my life, a special sincere thank you goes to our family, friends, and business associates to whom I owe a debt of gratitude that I can never repay.

Special thanks to my daughter, Autam Arner Urey, for her help in formatting and editing of *Longshot to a Miracle!*

Keep Smilin' & Never Give
UP!

xoxo always

Kassie Drexler

CONTENTS

Prologue 9

No Blood, No Foul 11
Life's Not Fair 13
No Guts, No Glory 16
Natural Athlete in Dress Shoes 19
3/4 Full 24
Tractor Races 29
Speedy 32
March 11 37
Heroic Efforts 55
Miracle Girl on Four 71
Team Red and White 89
The Arner Way 109
Habits 114
The Race Continues 117
The Infamous Kassie Scowl 129
Beautiful Contagious Smile 141
Eight 152
Subacute 158
Easter Sunday 178
One Hundred Steps 188
May 11 196
From Homecoming to Home Plate 199
Prayers Realized 210
Long Shot to a Miracle 219

Epilogue 223
Kassie's Chapter 243

I had caught our doctor, and family friend, as he finished with his final appointment. He was leaving immediately, reassuring me it was probably just a reaction from the medication he had prescribed, and that he would stop and get the counteractive medicine for Kassie on his way over. Even with the stop he had to make, it shouldn't take more than fifteen or twenty minutes. There was no way for him to know he would have to stop at multiple places before he could find what he needed to counteract Kassie's reaction; it was over forty-five minutes before he got here.

When he walked into our house, he looked at Kassie, our eleven-year-old daughter, and soberly asked, "How long has Kassie been breathing like that, like she can't catch her breath?"

While looking at his long and perplexed face, I stumbled through my mind trying to remember when Kassie's big sister, Autam, had come in to check on both of us. "I don't know…two hours…maybe three?"

The Narcan our doctor brought had no effect, and he hurriedly directed us to get Kassie to the ER while he called ahead so they would be ready for her. He looked me in the eyes and said, "Dave, *drive safe*, but don't waste any time getting her there."

His eyes told a story, and I knew my little girl was in trouble. My heart was pounding, yet I knew I had to stay calm.

I wanted to wave my magic wand and make everything all right. I wanted to slay the monsters and drive them from where they were causing harm, just like I had done hundreds of times before when she was scared or hurt. But she was unresponsive, and when I picked her up to carry her to the car, her body was limp. She did not stir.

My natural athlete, my track star who didn't know how to lose, did not even know the starting pistol had sounded. The race against the bacteria that was rapidly destroying her body and organs was already well under way. Kassie's opponent had cheated and left her quiet and sleeping at the starting line. Why hadn't I taught Kassie to use those damned starting blocks? You can be sure the bacteria used theirs, and they were striding out, only hungry for the win, and not caring about the outcome of their opponent.

As I was carrying Kassie to the car, Dawn, our neighbor from across the street, was out. Her older daughter, Courtney, was friends with Kassie, and they hung out all the time when Kassie wasn't at one of her numerous sporting events or at cheer practice. She asked if everything was okay, but she could tell it wasn't. I couldn't speak. All I could do was shake my head while fighting back tears, telling her with my eyes what no parent wants to ever think about, let alone say out loud. My Kassie, whose "life's glass" was always 3/4 full, was in trouble, and I knew in my soul it was bad. I thought, *This isn't how things are supposed to be*. I promised her that Daddy would never let anything bad happen to her. I "Daddy-Promised!" How would I ever explain not delivering on a Daddy Promise? How would I ever be able to live with myself again? As I put my seatbelt on, I thought, *Please let there be a clear path for our ten-minute drive to the hospital.*

When Kassie was five, I had been coaching my primary love, football, for ten years and was currently helping with the Modesto High School team. I tried to impress upon all three of our kids some very important life lessons from a very early age.

First of all, "No Blood, No Foul." This was heard often and the kids soon learned that little ouchies were no big deal. The kids would literally look to wherever they had just been hurt to see if they were bleeding before starting the tear factory. This was especially helpful with Kassie. Did I mention she could be dramatic?

From the beginning, we knew we had a pistol on our hands with Kassie. Our middle child was determined and headstrong on what she wanted, and wasn't afraid to ask for it, over and over again. And again, and again, and again. She also had a flair for the dramatic and was good at getting the last ounce of any emotion from any occurrence. I once caught her practicing crying in front of the mirror. She was quite a source of entertainment to all.

By this time, her athleticism was abundantly apparent. She also had a determined eight-year-old big sister to help her understand why you always gave your all, and it didn't matter whether it was a team sport, or on the playground, you always gave 100 percent. Kassie loved being at sporting events or plays, or any place where there were large groups of people doing things that she thought was fun, which was pretty much anything and everything.

Although Autam was a great role model to her little sister, it wasn't easy at the beginning for Autam. When Autam was two or three, she was very uncoordinated. She always had Vaseline gobbed on some place where she had biffed into a wall or smacked her head on a table or something else. We enrolled her in gymnastics to help with her motor skills. Most of the little kids were out there just having fun, but not Autam. She didn't like other kids doing things better than she could, so she dug in with a work ethic you don't normally find even with older kids. While the others were jumping into the foam pit for fun, Autam was working on her backbends. While the others were playing on the mini trampoline, she was practicing her backbend kickovers. It seemed like in no time at all, Autam was finally able to walk and chew gum without tripping.

In actuality, by the time Autam turned five, she had already been engrained with my philosophy on sports and had also inherited her mother's attribute to do things right the first time, so she became not only a great little athlete, but a great student as well. She applied that to her sports, and from the start, Autam was a student of the game. She was always wanting to learn and understand why things are done a certain way. Coaches love coachable kids, and they absolutely loved Autam.

We were the first of our friends to have children, and interestingly enough, Autam never learned how to crawl. Heck, she didn't even know she was supposed to crawl. Everyone she had seen was walking, so she skipped the crawling stage altogether. I still remember her befuddlement when we went to a party that had a child Autam's age. He was crawling around everywhere, and Autam couldn't figure out why the kid wouldn't stand up. She finally got down there with him and crawled around for a while but decided that was way too much work. I always wondered if her skipping crawling was why she was uncoordinated when she was young. No matter, with her hard work and dedication, she had certainly made up for any deficit that may have caused by the time she was eight years old.

My second important teaching was, "Life's Not Fair." Even though our youngest Steve, or Stevo as we called him, was two years younger than Kassie, he understood "Life's Not Fair" the best. With two older sisters who were tall and fast and aerodynamic, he had to learn to compensate for their speed with angles of pursuit and strength. While Kassie got the true benefit of a big sister, Stevo had the even greater benefit of two very diverse big sisters.

We had a yellow pedal coupe with turning hand controls that the kids had passed down to each other, and they all had great leg muscles because of it. The girls would go as fast as they could and power slide. As I have mentioned, the girls were built for speed. Stevo, on the other hand, was stocky and felt like a little chunk of concrete when you picked him up. By the time Stevo was old enough to reach the pedals, the coupe had many miles on it, but it was still in good shape. However, once Stevo had ended his time with it, the tires had been worn through, and he was trying to jump over things with it.

When we moved into our home in Modesto, California, Steve was just over one year old, and he was already bigger than the kid next door who was two. By the time they were riding trikes and big wheels, Stevo was making the front wheel spin and leaving skid marks up the driveway. When Stevo was three years old, he was smacking the ball over my head and halfway into the cul-de-sac. He was a strong kid, and I was very proud of my boy.

Although Stevo wasn't the same type of "athletic" as the girls, he was still well above average in comparison to kids his age. His biggest drawback was his heavy feet, combined with the fact he liked to watch his shadow as he ran. I was always worried that if he wasn't watching where he was running, he would certainly run into something, which of course he eventually did, another kid. Stevo came to an abrupt stop and sent the other kid flying through the air. I guess that was a sign of things to come. Stevo worked tirelessly to enhance his speed. He told me once, "Dad, I think my feet are made out of rocks. I'm too slow." When I asked him why he would think such a thing, he said, "I saw a big turtle pointing me out to his kids and laughing."

I couldn't help but laugh as I reassured him he would get faster if he kept working at it. Who says smart kids can't be funny?

Stevo was very bright, and he picked up academia quickly. Once, before Stevo was old enough to go to school, Lorrie was getting the girls out the door after quizzing them on their vocabulary words at the breakfast table.

When Lorrie came back, Stevo said, "Mom, is this right? Letters make sounds, you put letters together to make words, and put words together to make sentences?"

Somewhat astounded, Lorrie replied, "Yes, that's right."

And from that moment on, Stevo could read. Although Autam was our brainiac and a straight A student, she always said that Stevo was the smartest. He enjoyed playing different sports but only if there was action. He had no interest in a "standing around, waiting for something to happen" kind of sport. Stevo was a thrill-seeker extraordinaire.

The Coupe

NO GUTS, NO GLORY

My first job, the paying one, allowed me to be off a couple days through the week. Lorrie was able to stay at home with the kids and was very involved in their school and extracurricular activities. We had moved to Palmdale, California, by then, and we both got very involved in the town. I even cofounded an education foundation that teamed businesses up with the elementary school district to provide funding, materials, and mentorship to the students.

We enjoy doing things as a family. Lorrie and I both volunteered to help at the kids' school, and we became friends with the principal and teachers. Lorrie helped out in the classroom, became the chair for the school's PTA in charge of membership, and I helped out with the PE program. Once a year, the city held a citywide track meet at the high school for the fourth, fifth, and sixth graders. I was involved in helping to train our school's relay teams for all three grade levels, and in particular, practicing the proper distance to start running and handing off the batons cleanly for the relay. There was much debate about whether we should attempt to hand the batons off with a running start or from a standing start. Apparently, in previous years, the baton passing had been an issue, and some races had been lost due to being out of the run zone when the baton was actually passed or there had been numerous drops. As a result, for the last few years, our school had taken the batons from the standing start position instead of a running start. Passing batons takes a lot of practice time, and usually you had only one coach to do all events. There just hadn't been enough manpower to do the job right…until now.

Coach Haas and I had a great relationship. He respected that I wanted to spend time helping with physical education and teach the proponents of staying physically fit. We became great friends imme-diately. Usually, parents helped out in the academic classroom, not outside in the "real world" where athletics and the PE program itself were being cut to the bone because of money problems at the district and state levels.

Although Coach Haas chose which events the kids were going to compete in, he allowed me to choose how I wanted the relays to be done. I'm a "No Guts, No Glory" kind of guy, so running baton passes it was going to be.

One of the shortfalls about coaching your own kid is others always watching for special treatment. Everyone wants to be the last leg of the relay because you get to cross the finish line. Autam and one of her friends were very close in their times. Although Coach Haas made the decision to have Autam run anchor and her friend to run first, it was causing a bit of dissention from some. Autam and I decided that it would be better for the team for her to run first and let her friend run anchor.

At the track meet, the kids were all having fun, and we were cheering for our school. Kassie had pompoms and was generally hav-ing a great time in the stands with Stevo, Lorrie, and me. Kassie said she could hardly wait until next year when she would be old enough to do what Autam was doing. Stevo said he could hardly wait to have ice cream after the track meet. It finally came time for the final event of the day, the 400 relay. Autam came running up and said the girls had a meeting. They decided Autam and her friend should trade back spots, and have Autam run anchor. She was so excited she could barely contain herself. I had butterflies in my stomach, hoping the change in order of runners wouldn't screw up the handoffs we had worked so hard on. The race started, and the first baton pass went great, which put us in first place. The second pass went well, but we had dropped to a close third. The third pass also went great, but we had dropped to last place with Autam needing to make up about 20 meters on the leader. We were all jumping up and down in the stands when she rounded the corner to the straightaway, and Autam had closed the gap to half. Her eyes were as big around as silver dollars, and she had a huge smile on her face as she rounded turn four heading home. Kassie couldn't see because of everyone standing, so she started crawling up my leg to see what all the commotion was about. I tossed her on my shoulders, and we all watched Autam hit her stride, as she pulled up neck and neck on the leader with about 10 meters to go. We were screaming for Autam to go, and Kassie probably felt like she was on a bucking bronco as we watched Autam lean forward and win by a nose. Autam's entire team mobbed her at the finish line, and everyone was going crazy. I thought, *Of all the times not to have a video recorder!* I think that other than Autam, Kassie was the happiest, and she was telling everybody that Autam was her sister. Stevo even got caught up in the excitement and ran to give his big sister a hug, then very excitedly asked me if we got to go for ice cream now.

NATURAL ATHLETE
IN DRESS SHOES

P artially due to the intense "coaching" Autam had impressed upon Kassie early on, Kassie could not only outrun all the girls in her class, but all the boys in her class…and the class above, too…while wearing dress shoes.

Outside of sports, Kassie had a real easygoing demeanor. I used to describe Kassie as a little princess who just happened to have a linebacker's attitude lurking inside waiting to get out, providing of course that the linebacker could still wear a frilly dress.

Athletically, our two daughters were at the opposite ends of the spectrum, with Stevo being somewhere in the middle. Autam had developed a terrific work ethic because she was truly a student of every sport she played, while Kassie was more of a "natural" athlete and easily mastered all she tried. They both shared a near fanatical desire to win and were extremely competitive with each other, which their mother was not really pleased with at times.

Lorrie and I agreed it was important for our kids to be well-rounded, so we stressed both school and sports. I truly believe in sports and its benefits with kids. That is why I became a coach even before I had kids of my own. I jokingly referred to it as my second job. Honestly, there were times when I spent as much time at my second job as my first. But it was time well spent helping kids to realize their potential so they could get to their next level, whatever that may be. Sports teach you at an early age that even though you may be behind at a certain moment, whether it be in score or on a depth chart, there is always a chance that you can come back and win. By helping young people realize that hard work and practice will help them to accomplish their goals, it can also propel them to become better students in the classroom, better citizens, and overall, just better people. Couple that with the virtues of teamwork and following rules, it was determined we could put up with the competitiveness between our children.

Kassie always got the benefit of extra practices at home, too. When Kassie was seven years old, we had just signed Autam up to play girls' fast-pitch softball and Kassie to play T-ball. I was out in the front yard with Autam working on her slap bunt when I decided to give one of my best friends a call. T.C. was a teacher and a high school girls' fast-pitch coach in Phoenix, which is where we are from and where all three of the kids were born. I always tried to provide the best experience for my kids when they tried something new, and T.C. gave me some great tips. One of those tips was that if a girl can consistently get on base by slap bunting, she will be able to write her own ticket into college. That was very exciting to me, because as big of a proponent as I am for youth sports, I am an even larger proponent for using those sports to further your education for free. For that reason, we encouraged the kids do things they would continue doing as they got older.

Autam had played baseball the previous two years in Modesto before moving to Palmdale, because they didn't offer softball for the girls. Regarding sports back then, Autam really didn't like being thought of as a girl, because she said that nobody thought girls were any good at sports. So she tucked her long blonde hair up in her hat and played with the boys. Even though I knew Autam wasn't going to play baseball later, I felt it was a good tradeoff for fast-pitch softball, which she would play as she got older. The next year, we moved to Palmdale, and Autam was indeed playing fast-pitch. This is when I fell in love with the sport and knew I would want to help coach someday.

So there we were in the front yard putting T.C.'s newly acquired info to use, when out walks Kassie in her new T-ball uniform. She was wearing her sister's batting gloves and batting helmet from last year, all of which of course were too big. She was also wearing a pair of dress shoes because they matched her new Yankees uniform. As I mentioned before, my two girls are diverse. Autam tucked her hair up into her hat, while Kassie liked wearing frilly skirts and having her hair all done up and pretty. Kassie loved being a girl, acting like a girl, and looking like a girl. This is probably because when she grew up, she was going to be a princess, but that's a different story entirely. For now, Kassie had to just be daddy's little girl playing sports. As I said before, Kassie's athleticism was already apparent. After waiting an eternity for it to be her turn, about three or four more whiffs from Autam, Kassie strode in to take her turn. Mind you, she had never actually swung a real aluminum bat before. Everything to this point had been the big barreled plastic variety and ping-pong balls. I told her I would go get the tee for her to hit off, which drew a defiant No. She wanted to hit like the big girls. I agreed to let her try providing she would also use the tee later, because that was what she would be using in the games. She happily agreed and took her stance. Now I have to tell you, she was quite a sight to see. There she was with absolutely no idea of what she was doing, standing all wrong with the bat in the wrong position, her hands reversed, and this look upon her face that she had no idea what was about to happen, but whatever it was, she was going to meet it head on, with an air of defiance and confidence. I tossed the ball underhand to her, and she dang near took my head off with the ball coming right back at me. I chased the ball down the street, came back, worked on her stance, and showed her how to hold the bat. I tossed her a few more pitches, which she whacked, then got the tee out since that was part of the deal. After five or six smacks of the bat, it was Autam's turn again. Kassie had quelled her curiosity, so into the house she went to play with her Barbie dolls. Autam told me later that afternoon that Kassie was really going to be a good athlete and that Kassie was almost as fast as she was now. That was really saying something, because Autam was the fastest girl in her class. By the way, Kassie only played one year of T-ball and went right into fast-pitch softball. By then, she enjoyed wearing cleats almost as much as dress shoes. She would even go to school in cleats sometimes, providing they matched what she was wearing.

Kassie batting practice

Big girl dress up

Baseball in Palmdale, CA

1997 Shredder Team—The Football Family, Mom—Team Mom, Dad—
Head Coach, Autam—Cheer Coach, Stevo—Player, Kassie—Cheerleader

3/4 FULL

Most people look at life like the glass is always either half-full or half-empty. Kassie looked at life like the glass was always 3/4 full, with a chance there was more to be added. She was very well-liked because of this and had multitudes of friends. Although she liked being the girly girl, she also loved getting dirty and digging in the dirt looking for cool-looking bugs and turning over rocks to see what she could find. She would sometimes sneak off to the pond with Autam and find tadpoles and other similarly cool things to bring home and keep. When she was about seven or so, she even shared these fine attributes of dirt digging and bug finding with one of her friends who had clearly never come close to the dirt before. To her poor mother's shock and dismay, when she came to pick her daughter up from an afternoon playing with Kassie, both girls were covered in dirt from head to toe. Lorrie says she can still see the mother's face now, straining not to cry out, "Didn't you supervise these girls at all?" Of course, Lorrie was looking back as if saying, *What? It's just dirt*. Soon after, the mom became very good friends with Lorrie. She even helped Lorrie when she was the Brownie Leader, going camping and doing field trips. What a learning experience that must have been.

People say the middle child takes time to find their own identity. With Kassie, I don't think that was ever the case. She acted and thought bigger than life. There was nothing she couldn't do; there was nothing she couldn't be. She followed her big sister around and wanted to do everything Autam did. With Kassie's natural ability at athletics, I would constantly warn her that she couldn't get lazy. Hard work and practice always overcomes natural ability sooner or later. If she truly wanted to be the best at something when she got older, she would have to do more than just show up to win. This was something that Kassie was destined to find out; excruciatingly, heartbreakingly so.

Before Kassie was ten years old, she really didn't have anyone her age who could push her to become better, so she tended to practice with older kids her sister's age. All the way up to when Kassie got sick at eleven, she was really unequaled in her own age bracket. She set school record after school record for the running events, short and long. If you wanted Kassie to do something, all you had to do was tell her that nobody had done whatever activity it was in such and such time or in such and such space. She was extremely motivated to be the best. She would set her sights and somehow get there, all the while never having to work really hard at it. All the way up until eleven years old, Kassie had never lost a running race with her peers. And at least some of the time, she continued to do it wearing dress shoes and dresses.

It was a very difficult decision to leave Palmdale and move back to Phoenix, but the time had come and we were tired of being alone in California. All of my family and a lot of Lorrie's family lived in Phoenix, and we are a very, very family-oriented group. It was difficult to leave, but it was more difficult for us to stay and see less of our loved ones. We had been gone over six years, and the kids were now thirteen, ten, and eight. I got a job offer in Phoenix to start February 1, and away I went. We decided Lorrie would stay behind with the kids to finish the school year. They followed me to our new home a couple of months later; albeit with bittersweet feelings from Autam, who had really fallen in with a great group of friends.

Palmdale had been on a year-round school schedule and Phoenix wasn't, so upon their arrival, the kids settled in to finish out their school year again. There was a benefit however, especially for Kassie. She got to do another Field Day at school and enter a bunch of events, which of course she won, setting records in most every event she entered at her new school. We had moved in with my parents while we searched for a home to purchase, so it was pretty cool for me to have the kids going to the same school I had attended. One of the best parts was that some of the same teachers and coaches were still there finishing out their careers from when I was there twenty-five years earlier. Kassie's fourth grade teacher, Miss Marbaugh, had been my sixth grade teacher.

My parents, my older sister, and I had moved to Phoenix from Oklahoma the summer before my sixth grade year. Miss Marbaugh was my first teacher in Arizona. My older brother Steve, or Uncle Steve as everyone referred to him later because of his younger namesake, was in the military. He used to kiddingly say that we waited to move to Phoenix until he was gone and didn't even tell him we were moving.

Miss Marbaugh was a great teacher and tried to keep the other kids from making too much fun of me and my twang of an accent. All in all, I really didn't mind too much. I was somewhat of a jester and enjoyed the attention most of the time.

My PE coach was still there also, Coach Cameron. Although both had aged in the twenty-plus years since I had seen them, they were still the same people as I remembered. Coach Cameron was very impressed with Autam and Stevo but took a special interest in Kassie because of her speed. He joked with me that all of my kids must have taken after their mother because they were all better athletes than I was at their age. He encouraged me to find a track team Kassie could get involved with to help hone her skills and also to help prevent her from losing interest in track before she peaked.

Summer arrived and we took Coach Cameron's advice and entered all three kids into the Hershey's track meet that was in Glendale. My ulterior motive was to get accurate times for them all. The competition was broken down by age, in two-year brackets as of a certain date. Kassie said it wasn't fair she was born at the end of December and she had to race girls who would be up to two years older than her.

In response, I pulled out the tried and true, "Life's not fair, honey, get used to it. Just go do your best."

She playfully protested as she always did, flashing her beautiful contagious smile, telling me she didn't like that rule and skipped off to run in her event. I didn't have the heart to explain most of these girls were actually almost three years older than she was, because of how they broke down the ages.

When they took to the starting line, Kassie looked like a kid running against adults. They were all at least a head taller and ran on track teams. Kassie had never used starting blocks before, so when they took off, Kassie didn't get as good a start as the others. She started off in last place, and the other girls were really striding out. Then all of a sudden, it was like Kassie kicked it into another gear I had never seen. She started to close on the group and pulled within a few yards of them at the finish line. Kassie was all bent out of shape because she didn't win and was embarrassed she came in last. I had to remind her that these girls were turning thirteen and she had just turned ten. It didn't matter to her that they were nearly three years older, she wanted to run against them again.

I explained it didn't work like that, and she would have to look forward to next time.

With that, I got the infamous Kassie scowl—the look she gave when she felt she had been wronged. She sarcastically sang, "I know, Daddy, life's not fair," and off she went with her brother and sister to find some cotton candy.

Later that day, I found out that she had run a 13.81 in the hundred-meter dash as a ten-year-old. She may not have been happy, but I was.

Miss Marbaugh

Once school ended, we had a lot of time to spend together as a family again. While Lorrie was driving one day, she saw something she thought the kids would enjoy doing, tractor racing. It was an event that Kmart was putting on called "Kids Race Against Drugs." They had a course laid out in one of the Kmart parking lots, and the kids got to drive and race riding lawn mowers. Each of the kids did well, but Kassie actually won the event, which came with a nifty trophy. The coolest part though was the grand prize trip to Disneyworld and being able to represent Arizona at the "Kids Race Against Drugs" Riding Lawnmower Nationals in Fort Lauderdale, Florida. Lorrie hated the fact that because of my job, I never got to go on trips with the kids or do any of the fun stuff, but that was the way of my profession. As a result, Lorrie and Kassie headed off to beautiful, sunny Florida for an all-expense paid trip to the Nationals and Disneyworld.

When they arrived, the sponsors of the event bought everyone warm clothes, because sunny Florida was having a cold front move through, and what they told everyone to pack didn't work out so well. Kassie thought that was another nice little perk, new clothes! They both had a great time and got to meet Kathy Ireland and a few other celebrities. As they walked into Disneyworld, Kassie was petting the Clydesdale horse's nose, when somehow her hand got in the horse's mouth while it was chewing on something. Lorrie looked down, saw Kassie's face, and immediately got the guy's attention who was watching the horse. I think the guy about passed out when he jerked the horse to get Kassie's hand out. Everyone expected a bloody stub, but apparently the horse could tell it was her fingers and stopped chewing. He just happened to stop chewing while Kassie's fingers were still between his teeth. Aside from the bellowing that then ensued and a few slightly chewed fingers, no real damage was done. She told me on the phone when she looked at her fingers there was no blood, and she tried to abide by the "No Blood, No Foul" rule, but she couldn't help crying because it hurt so bad. I told her we could overlook the rule violation this time due to extenuating circumstances. I always got a kick out of Kassie telling me how something got hurt, and while she was telling the story, she would start crying as if it had just happened again. Did I mention that she has a flair for the dramatic, and that she was a great source of entertainment to all? Little did we know that Kassie's tractor racing escapades would play such an important role in the very near future.

Kids Race Against Drugs K-Mart Tractor Race

Tournament Win—Competitive Fast Pitch

SPEEDY

We decided the girls were going to try out for club softball. Some of the girls' friends played, and both wanted to give it a try. Club is a much more intense version of the game than what the girls were used to. It demanded a lot of time for practice and the entire weekend for the series of games, something Lorrie was not really thrilled about. There were actual tryouts, and a lot of girls trying to make the team. Autam was trying out for the fourteen or younger age bracket, while Kassie tried out for the twelve or younger bracket. Fortunately for both girls, even though they had never played club before, they both made their teams. Both girls learned a tremendous amount from this experience, and their skill level really improved. This was by far the most intense sport the girls had been involved with, and the mentality was that winning was *the* most important thing. I always stressed to the kids that winning was important, but tempered that with the fact that they were still learning, and as long as they were getting better, they were on the right track. One of the phrases I liked was, "If it wasn't important whether you win or lose, why keep score?" So even though I raised my kids with a competitive spirit and a desire to win, club softball was an eye-opening experience of what to expect once they got to high school. I have to admit Kassie's coach was a bit extreme, and some of the girls consistently had tears in their eyes after practice. Kassie usually just left mad because she felt she was underutilized for her abilities. If I only had a dollar for each time "Life's Not Fair" was uttered while Kassie played on that team.

When Lorrie and I were first married and thinking about having children, my buddies would always kid me and ask what I would do if my kids weren't interested in sports. Would I force them to do things they had no interest in? What if I had a boy and he didn't want to play football? All of these things made great conversation while downing a few Jack Daniels, especially because all of my friends were jocks that played multiple sports. I always thought of myself as being fairly athletic and talented, but all my friends were more talented than I ever was. They also took great joy in firing "what ifs" at me. Of course, at that time, it was a foregone conclusion, at least in my mind, that our kids would undoubtedly be superstars. How could they not? I had all the talented coaches any kid would ever need sitting in my family room. I knew that if my kids wanted to play something, I would be able to enlist the help of any of the guys with a phone call. However, through much debate, I determined that on the off chance our kids would rather play the piano than run the bases or score touchdowns, piano lessons it would be.

As the years rolled along, our lives became busier and busier. We had moved to a different state, my friends got married, had kids of their own, and we saw each other less and less. However, I never lost my core group of friends. If there was ever anything important, good or bad, we kept each other in the loop.

After a year of club softball and the rigors that put us through, we decided that while it was a great opportunity for the girls, and the experience and coaching they received was exceptional, it was just too time consuming.

Kassie remained busy doing what Kassie was always doing, which was absolutely everything! She was playing basketball on her school's team, again a sport she had never really played before other than in the driveway. She was cheerleading for Stevo's football team, she was running, and she had just started to play fast-pitch softball for a new non-club team, the Panthers. Kassie had an uncanny ability to make friends quickly. She had friends spread out all over the place, doing all different sorts of activities. She never had to worry about having someone to play with, that was for certain. Kassie was blind to popularity, looks, impediments, and cliques. She truly had only one litmus test, and that was whether or not you were nice to others, as well as whether you got along with all of Kassie's other friends.

Her new softball coach was Charlie LeMaster, and we all liked him from the start. Charlie was a big guy and had been coaching fast-pitch softball for a while. He also had a daughter on the team. Kassie and Brooke quickly became friends. Coach Charlie was likable and knew how to get the best results out of his team. He was a strong positive reinforcement coach to the girls, and our styles meshed very well. I did have to warn him that I coached Kassie to be very aggressive on base running, and she might turn his salt and pepper hair prematurely gray. Kassie was an absolute terror on the bases and gave the opposing team's catchers and pitchers fits, because of her speed. She almost dared them to try and throw her out. Did I mention that she was a great source of entertainment for all?

At the end of one of her practices during the first week on her new team, the girls were being timed on how fast they could get around the bases. One of the things I really liked about Coach Charlie was that even when the girls were competing against each other, he required everyone to root for the girl performing and to shout encouragement for them to do their best. Charlie had said if everyone participated and tried their best, they would get a treat at the end of practice. They had a girl returning to the team who was really quick and the team had nick named her "Wheels." She went first and set the time for the rest of the girls to try and beat. She ran the bases fast like a cat and was very smooth all the way around. When she crossed home plate, she had bettered her time from the previous year, so the rest of her teammates were primed for a showdown. Each of the girls tried their best but were unable to match Wheels's efforts. Kassie was toward the end of the line of the girls waiting to run. When it was her turn, she walked to the starting position with this huge grin on her face and was smacking bubble gum. Charlie looked at me from first base with a grin and said, "Well, she doesn't lack in confidence, does she?" We laughed, and I kind of shrugged my shoulders exclaiming that I didn't know where she got it from.

Kassie took off with her teammates cheering her on. She clipped the inside corners of the bases with her outside foot and never lost stride. When she crossed home plate, she was going full speed and skidded into the backstop with a pile of dust following her. Did I mention that she had a flair for the dramatic?

The girls were all hopping and high-fiving each other when Coach Charlie announced that Kassie had beaten Wheels's time. Everyone was in disbelief.

Kassie got kind of cocky and was talking some smack like, "Oh yeah, that's why they call me Speedy," and strutted around like she had just won the Olympics.

I looked at Charlie and said, "You'll have to excuse us for a few minutes."

I was standing in the third base coaching box where I had been shouting encouragement for the girls as they rounded second. I motioned for Kassie to come over to me and asked another parent who was close by to take over for a bit as I walked into left field. Kassie came bebopping over all excited about her latest accomplishment.

I told her very sternly, "That type of behavior is not going to be tolerated by me or Coach Charlie ever!" Kassie looked at me like a deer in the headlights. I explained in a very low voice, "Why don't you try putting the shoe on the other foot? Imagine how you would feel if someone new came in and beat you in front of all of your friends then acted in the manner that you just did. How would you feel?"

She thought for a moment, then responded that she hadn't thought of it like that. She was just kidding around being goofy and that she was very sorry.

I told her that wasn't the way it came off, and she needed to go do something about it.

She nodded and ran back to her team.

Coach Charlie had just finished with the timings. He was talking with all the girls in a circle when Kassie ran up to them. Charlie teasingly thanked "Speedy" for deciding to join the rest of the team, which caused everyone to laugh.

In typical Kassie fashion, she cocked her head and said, "Yeah, no prob, Coach," while popping a bubble and flashing that big contagious smile.

All the girls laughed again, then Kassie turned serious. Kassie looked right at Wheels and said she was sorry for acting out when Coach Charlie announced her time and that she didn't mean anything by it. Kassie then apologized to the entire team and told them all how happy she was to be playing with them.

They all were kind of quiet, not really knowing how to react when Wheels broke the ice and said, "No problem! We're glad you're here. You're gonna help us win some games this year."

Charlie looked at me and smiled. Later while we were carrying the equipment to the truck, he told me I had quite a girl, a real class act, and that he was awfully happy to have us on his team. From that moment on, the team had great chemistry, and all the girls got along really well. There were no egos, just lots of fun.

Kassie continued to work hard with her new team, while practicing for her school basketball team and running track. Ever since she was a baby, Kassie was the healthiest kid ever. In the eleven years since she had been born, it seemed she hardly ever got sick. Mind you, she would bring the germs home and get the rest of us sick, but she always seemed to be able to shrug it off and just keep on trucking. Winter was turning to spring in Phoenix, and the weather was just perfect. However, due to the changing of the seasons, it had gone from cold to warm a few times over the last couple of weeks. Autam and I were fighting off a cold and were generally just feeling yucky, but to everyone's surprise, Kassie had actually gotten really sick.

Kassie had been back and forth a couple of times with Lorrie to the doctor because she had flu symptoms, and she just couldn't shake it. She was beginning to get dehydrated by the constant vomiting, and she had started getting a sharp pain in her chest. Our doctor proscribed a pretty heavy-duty medication to help Kassie rest and figured she had probably pulled a muscle from having dry heaves. I have to admit that sometimes it was hard to tell how bad things really were with Kassie because of her dramatic flair. This time though, we could tell without question that she was not faking how bad she felt.

Although I was not feeling great, I didn't feel so sick that I couldn't go into work. Now that the kids were older and all in school, Lorrie was back in the workforce but decided she should take a couple days off to take care of our two sick girls. When my days off came, Lorrie headed back to work to catch up on what she had missed. That morning, as Lorrie was getting ready for work, Kassie was acting kind of goofy. It finally seemed she was getting to be herself again. Lorrie plopped her on the couch after getting her to eat something for the first time in days. I finally came stumbling out and plopped on the other couch next to the one Kassie was on, so I could listen and help get her some water or anything else that was necessary. Autam stayed in her room and was sleeping in so that she could get well and be back to school the following day. Lorrie gave Kassie the medicine that had been prescribed and then told me Kassie would probably sleep until she got home. Lorrie is a great mother and always puts her kids first. She also knows that when I get sick, I am a big wuss; not only would she have the girls to take care of, but me, too, so she was only going to work a half day.

I woke briefly a couple times to Autam checking in on us. She asked why Kassie was breathing so funny, almost like she was gasping for air and moaning. Autam asked, "Is Kassie really that sick or is she just being Kassie with all the drama?"

I told her no, that Kassie was asleep and she must really be in a lot of pain for her to be acting that way while she's asleep. I comforted Autam with the fact that Kassie had seen the doctor twice in as many days and that Kassie was taking some heavy-duty medications to help her sleep. I told her not to worry, that her little sister was going to be fine, and for her to go back to bed to continue getting some rest. I hadn't noticed that Kassie's fingers and toes were beginning to turn blue like Autam had.

A very short time later, Lorrie got home, and we tried to rouse Kassie to get her to try and eat something and to give her some additional meds. I sensed something was terribly wrong. I had been around sports and taken enough emergency sports medicine classes to know Kassie wasn't reacting to stimulation like she should. I got a flashlight to check her pupils, and they didn't react. I ran to the phone to call our doctor. He and I had been friends for nearly ten years, and he was like a brother to me; our families even went on vacations together. He treated my kids like they were his kids. I broke down on the phone while telling him that something was terribly wrong. He assured me that Kassie was probably just having a reaction to the medication he had prescribed, and that he would stop and get some Narcan to counteract the meds she was taking.

I felt fortunate that I had caught our family friend, and doctor, as he was finishing the paperwork from his final appointment. He said he could leave immediately, and that even with the stop he had to make, it shouldn't take more than fifteen or twenty minutes. We just needed to sit tight, and he would be there shortly. Minutes seemed like hours. Our doctor had trouble finding what he needed for Kassie, so it took him longer to get there than he anticipated.

When he walked in, he looked at Kassie and soberly asked, "How long has Kassie been breathing like that, like she can't catch her breath?"

I stumbled through my mind trying to remember when Autam had come in the last time. I didn't know…two hours…maybe three?

The Narcan our doctor brought had no effect, and he directed us to get Kassie to the ER at the nearby hospital. He looked me squarely in the eyes and said, "Dave, *drive safe*, but don't waste any time getting her there."

His eyes told the story, and I knew my little girl was in trouble. My heart was pounding, yet I knew I had to stay calm. I wanted to wave my magic wand and make everything all right; I wanted to slay the monsters hiding in Kassie and drive them from where they were causing harm. But she was unresponsive, and when I picked her up to carry her to the car, her body was limp, and she did not stir. My natural athlete, my track star who didn't know how to lose, did not even know the starting pistol had sounded. The race against the bacteria that was rapidly destroying her body and organs was already well under way. Kassie's opponent had cheated and left her quiet and sleeping at the starting line. Why hadn't I taught Kassie to use those damned starting blocks? You can be sure the bacteria used theirs, and they were striding out, only hungry for the win, and not caring about the outcome of their opponent.

As I was carrying Kassie to the car, our neighbor from across the street was out. Her older daughter, Courtney, was friends with Kassie, and they hung out all the time when Kassie was at home. She asked if everything was okay, but she could tell it wasn't. All I could do was shake my head while fighting back tears, telling her with my eyes what no parent wants to ever think about. My Kassie, whose "life's glass" was always three-fourths full, was in trouble, and I felt in my soul it was bad.

When I got to the ER at the hospital, I carried Kassie in and exclaimed that we had a possible accidental narcotics overdose, and we needed help now! They took us immediately into a room, then someone came in and asked if we were the Arners. When we said yes, they whisked us away to another room. They were ready for us, thanks to our doctor calling in to prewarn them. They had a STAT room already prepared with about a dozen people at the ready, and they went to work on Kassie without hesitation. They cut Kassie's clothes off her and began trying to determine why she wasn't getting oxygen.

They pulled Lorrie and me out of the room and began a series of questions regarding family history, if she was allergic to anything, what happened to Kassie, did she fall or was she being punished before she wouldn't wake up? I knew what they were driving at, and my head about exploded at the thought they may think I could have hurt my Kassie. I answered all questions as best as I could. I explained about how she was sick, she was involved in sports, she hadn't said anything about getting hit in the head to me, and no, I had not done anything to make this situation worse. We were all grasping for straws to figure out why, or what, or how. All I could think was, "Please help Kassie." All I wanted to say was, "Throw me in jail if you want to, but please do not take a second away from what you are doing right now to save my little girl."

Kassie was not producing enough oxygen to support her life. They took an X-ray of her lungs, which showed that Kassie's left lung was completely compromised with fluid. I still couldn't understand why there wasn't enough oxygen though. I thought, *People can live with one lung*. Why was Kassie nonresponsive? In my head, I screamed, *This shouldn't be happening, why doesn't anyone know what's causing this? It isn't fair!* I immediately froze in my tracks. This little voice deep in my brain said, "Life's not fair," almost so faint I couldn't hear it. But I could feel it. It was like a freight train jumping the tracks in my heart. I thought, *Oh my god! Life's not fair!* I knew what that meant. That meant that life was getting ready to deal a learning lesson. That meant we were in far bigger trouble than I had ever dared to think about before now. That meant we had better get going before it was too late. Her tiny opponents were already halfway to the first turn, and Kassie was still at the starting line.

The hospital ER quickly ran out of options to try, and they told us that Kassie's best bet was to get to Phoenix Children's Hospital as soon as possible, where they were more qualified to figure out Kassie's situation. I asked if they really thought it would be necessary to transfer her to a different hospital completely across town. It was now rush hour in Phoenix, and I figured there would be at least an hour-long drive to PCH. When I mentioned it was rush hour, they looked at me like, "Hello, is anybody home in there?" They then explained that Kassie was to be airlifted; the chopper was en route and would arrive in minutes. Kassie was being prepped for the ride now, and there would be no time wasted in getting Kassie to Phoenix Children's Hospital. The nurse then looked directly at me, held my hand, and said, "I promise, she'll get the best treatment possible on the way." The urgency was direct, but the compassion was excruciating. She gave us directions to the children's hospital and assured us that Kassie would be there once we arrived. Lorrie and I blinked at each other, trying to absorb everything that had happened, and that was still happening. It was a blur. Wasn't it just this morning that Kassie was acting silly and looked to be on the road to recovery? We had no idea that the silly and goofy performance witnessed this morning was because her brain was being starved of life-giving oxygen.

*****

On the car ride to Phoenix Children's Hospital, Lorrie and I quickly stopped at home to get a few things for Kassie's stay at the hospital. We knew that she was going to be there for at least a little while, and she would need something comfortable to wear. My parents lived just down the street, and Lorrie and I switched places so that I could let them know what was going on.

When we moved back to Phoenix from California about a year before, we lived with my parents for a number of months until we could find a place of our own. My parents loved having us around and didn't seem to mind seven people in a 1,500-square-foot, three-bedroom home. We ended up purchasing a home less than a block from my parents to live in until we found the right location to build a new house.

Word had already traveled down to my folks. When I walked into their house, my parents were in the kitchen and could see I was on the edge. I was having trouble speaking, but I got out that something was wrong with Kassie, and she was really sick. Then I sobbed that they were airlifting her to Phoenix Children's Hospital because she wasn't getting enough oxygen. We needed to get down there as soon as we could. As I walked toward them, my mom came over to me and gave me a hug. I heard them call out that they knew Kassie would be okay, as I started out the door to run the rest of the way up the street to my house. I rushed through the door as Lorrie was talking to the kids. Grandma and Grandpa were going to come over to watch them, while Mom and Dad went to see Kassie. This all took Stevo very much by surprise. He was at school when this all went down, and because of his age, he didn't fully grasp the severity of the situation. What he saw was that his mommy and daddy were visibly shaken, and that got his attention.

When we finally arrived at Phoenix Children's Hospital, our emotions were on our sleeves, because of the gridlocked traffic and because of Kassie's obvious predicament. We sat down with Dr. Robin Lax. She was the person who was given the duty of informing us of the situation and what they were doing to help Kassie. She started out by saying that Kassie was a very sick little girl and that everything possible was being done to help her. Lorrie and I sat there nodding and hanging on her every word, trying to fully understand all that she was saying. She explained that Kassie was not getting enough oxygen to support her own life. In the time it took for Kassie to be flown from one hospital to the other, she now had one lung completely compromised, and her second lung was already beginning to fill. She then said they would do everything they could to keep her comfortable, and she would make sure that Kassie's dignity would not be jeopardized.

Lorrie was asking her some questions, but I wasn't listening. I was thinking repeatedly, *Kassie's dignity would not be jeopardized... hmm... Kassie's dignity would not be jeopardized.* I continued thinking, *That doesn't sound good. I don't like that she said that. This bothers me, and I don't like that she said that!* I focused back in as Dr. Lax was finishing up from Lorrie's question. She was wondering if we wanted to have Kassie's brother and sister come down, as it might be the right time. I wondered if they had noticed I wasn't listening. It took all the gumption I could muster to ask what needed to be asked, to ask a question that no father wants to ever ask.

I looked into Dr. Lax's eyes. "Dr. Lax, it sounds like you are saying..." I stammered. "Are you saying Kassie is going to die?"

Dr. Lax looked at me and said that there was a real strong possibility Kassie would not be able to survive the night.

I was stunned. All of a sudden, it felt like I had just taken a shot to the head by a heavyweight boxer. I heard a question being asked about what Kassie's chances could be, but did I ask that, or was it Lorrie?

I focused up again trying to shake the cobwebs from my brain to hear her respond, "Kassie has about a five percent chance of making it through the night," and that she was very sorry.

Another blow to the head had just landed like a scud missile with pinpoint accuracy. It hit me in the brain, but I felt it in my heart.

That instant, that very instant, was to be the last time in my life where I could have a faint belief that no matter what, I would always be able to protect my children from anything that got tossed our way. Me! Kassie's daddy! I was the one that "Daddy Promised" hundreds of times, "Daddy would never let anything really bad happen." I would always be there to chase monsters from their closets or out from under their beds. I would always slay the dragons! I would scare the ghosts! I would be the one who stood guard every night so they could sleep without worry. Daddy would be there, and only Daddy could fix "Life's Not Fair" with a smile and a wink.

Never again would I be able to say "Life's Not Fair" and not remember all the times that Kassie told me she didn't like that rule before flashing that beautiful contagious smile and got on with whatever she was conquering. Never again could I be awake and not feel the guilt only a daddy can feel about making unkept promises to innocents in his charge. Never again would I be me in that same kind of way.

Dr. Lax left us to be with ourselves. I was trying to hold it together, to be strong, to be a man, but I couldn't; my Kassie was dying, and I was a basket case. I cried uncontrollably and prayed, as if I had any right to ask God for anything. While I was praying, I was thinking how unworthy I was to ask for His help. Sure I believed in God, but did I go to church other than when it was obligatory like on Easter and Christmas? Did I even go last year at all? Who was I to ask for a special favor of God? I felt alone, and I felt helpless. I felt helpless to do anything to help Kassie. Then a thought quickly entered my mind, *What about my promise?* I had made a promise that I needed to keep. I finished my prayer asking for strength to get through this, asking strength for my family and loved ones, and asking for strength be given to Kassie, so she could survive long enough for the rest of us to figure something out. I asked that God's will be for Kassie to live. Then I asked for God to be with me and to help me find a way to save Kassie.

I felt like such a hypocrite, and I loathed myself for it, but I didn't have time for that. It was time to focus and do something. It was time for "Daddy mode." First things first, Kassie needed to know I was there. She needed to know she had to fight. She needed to know the race wasn't over. She needed to know someone believed she could still win. She needed to know…that I believed.

*****

While Lorrie and I had been talking with Dr. Lax, my parents arrived at the hospital followed shortly by my brother and sister. Other family and friends were beginning to filter in as well, and we filled them in on the situation. We asked everyone to pray for Kassie and to call anyone they knew who would pray for Kassie. There was a shift change going on, so there were many doctors and nurses in the ICU working. I began to notice through my tunnel vision that there was no eye contact toward us from anyone. Chances are, they did not want to let anyone know the truth that Kassie would more than likely die soon. I thought to myself how difficult it would be for me to work in this environment. I get misty eyed at movies when a kid or animal gets hurt, a trait that I had inherited from my mom and was sometimes embarrassed about.

When I finally got to see Kassie for the first time since arriving at PCH, she was surrounded by nurses and doctors. Dr. Tellez came over and introduced himself. He explained that they were trying to get Kassie's oxygen saturation levels up and that her lungs were under attack from something. They had drawn blood and were waiting for the results. I asked how long that would take, and he said normally twenty-four hours. He then confirmed that we had been briefed on Kassie's prognosis before reiterating we did not have twenty-four hours. He also explained that he had asked the tech to look at it immediately and give an opinion. The tech felt it was Strep Pneumococcal Pneumonia, a highly aggressive bacterial infection that takes only two hours to produce the effect regular pneumonia causes in twenty-four hours. He then explained that strep pneumo is something that can be susceptible to basic penicillin, and that Kassie had been given a major dose of the drug to try and stop the spread of the infection. He said that if a shot of penicillin was like a bullet, Kassie received the equivalent to a cannon blast. He told me that Kassie was strong, and he could tell by the fact she was still alive that she was a fighter. He then explained that strep pneumo can be fatal because of how fast it grows in the body. Sometimes, a patient dies before they figure out they are really sick and come into the hospital. He then told us that Kassie's organs had already began shutting down, and that even though Kassie was fighting, we might want to consider having anyone who is close to Kassie to come down so they can say good-bye. I could tell that Dr. Tellez had said those words before, but that fact didn't make it any easier for him.

As I looked at Kassie while stroking her hair and holding her hand, I continued to tell her that Daddy and Mommy were here, and we weren't going to leave. I told her that she needed to fight really hard, harder than she had ever fought before. I couldn't help but think of our first rule, "No Blood, No Foul." I closely inspected Kassie's nearly lifeless body, already turning to gray—the color of death. There was no blood flowing from a wound. There wasn't even so much as a trickle of red to wipe clean. I gently whispered in Kassie's ear, "No Blood, No Foul, baby. No Blood, No Foul." But there was no response, no dramatic crocodile tears to wipe away before helping her up to her feet and sending her back into the fray with a couple of pats on the butt for good luck. Just deafening silence and the slight recognition that there were loud alarms going off from the monitors connected to Kassie.

*****

Kassie's oxygen levels were dropping, even with her being on 100 percent oxygen. The nurses feverishly worked their magic, getting her to stabilize for a few moments before she slipped a little deeper into the abyss that was consuming her by the second. While more and more alarms sounded, more and more family and friends continued to show up at the hospital. Before long, over forty people were there praying and conveying their good thoughts and wishes for Kassie. My sister's friend, Debbie McMahon, was one of the people there that night. Debbie had been a friend of our family for almost as long as we had lived in Arizona. She was another of our friends who thought of our parents as if they were her own parents, and she had truly become a part of our family. Debbie is very perceptive and gifted with the ability to see things that most people cannot. I went to her and asked what she thought.

She said as crowded as the room seemed to us, it was even more crowded with the other people present that we couldn't see.

I could only assume she meant there were family members and friends who had already passed away watching over Kassie and giving her support.

She then said something I will never forget. She said, "David, I truly don't know what the outcome of this is going to be. On one hand, I see Kassie as a young adult riding horses with her long hair blowing in the wind, and on the other hand, I don't see anything but fog. I don't know what that means, but I can tell you that Kassie is a very special girl because along with the others in there I told you about, she has two guardian angels sitting above her head watching over her. Keep up the faith and keep praying for a miracle."

My heart skipped a beat, and I thought to myself about the power of prayer and how magnificent everyone's love was for Kassie. I told everyone there with us that their prayers were working and asked again for them to please call their friends to help. I didn't realize to what degree they had already been doing just that, starting before they had even arrived at the hospital. Our loved ones continued calling their friends, asking them to call their friends, who were asking their friends to call their friends. A prayer chain was immediately being spread across our nation from Hawaii to Florida. Someone had put a general call to prayer for Kassie Charree Arner onto the internet and that was now going worldwide. People were praying for Kassie who didn't even know her. They were praying for a little girl whom their friend's friend of a friend's friend had never even met before. They were praying for someone's "daddy's little girl"…my little girl. If Kassie were to have a chance to make it through the night, every prayer would be needed. I only *hoped* that we wouldn't fall one prayer short of some imaginary number needed to warrant a miracle. And then I *prayed* that we wouldn't fall one prayer short to save Kassie. I hoped if there was a light that showed up in heaven representing the person being prayed for, Kassie's light would be so bright that it looked like the sun. I hoped for a light so bright that God himself would have to take notice. A light so bright that maybe he could overlook how unworthy Kassie's daddy was and only see how worthy Kassie was of His own personal attention.

*****

Our doctor and his family were there at the bedside. Don was grasping tightly onto Kassie's hands, arms, chest, legs, first one, then another, and then another, concentrating and sending as much healing energy as he could to her. I asked him to take a walk with me. We took the elevator downstairs, then walked in silence for a while until I finally stopped. I didn't want to, but I had to ask my friend for his opinion on the situation. I needed to know what he thought, because I trusted him and I knew he would tell me whatever he thought was true. I needed to hear it from him; I needed to be sure of what was happening.

As we looked at each other like brothers, he said to me, "Dave, I think she's just too far gone. Her organs have begun shutting down, and there's nothing that can be done medically to help." He looked at me with tears in his eyes and stated, "Dave, I have always taken care of your kids just like they were my own, why did this have to happen to Kassie? Why did it have to happen?"

I looked at him, and he could see I already knew all of what he said. We cried in each other's arms together; not like a doctor consoling a patient, but like two men who had lost something very precious that couldn't be replaced.

As we composed ourselves and went back up to Kassie's room, I thought, *How could this have happened to Kassie? I don't think she has ever really been sick a day in her life. How could Kassie be lying in a bed upstairs fighting for her life, perhaps taking her final breath? How could this truly be happening to my little girl that loves life so much?* I knew there were no answers; the only thing I could be sure of was that I had to do something, anything. I had to be Kassie's daddy. She would expect me to keep fighting, just like I had taught her and expected her to keep fighting. I had always relentlessly pounded it into our kids' heads that you never stop trying, you continue doing what you are doing until the very end. You don't stop giving 100 percent until the final whistle or the final out, not until it's over; and as of right now, it wasn't over, because Kassie was still fighting. That was the attitude I had instilled in the kids, which had proven effective many times over when they were behind at something and then came back to win. Perseverance and fortitude of effort were paramount. Kassie was still laboring to make a comeback with every breath she stole away from death itself. She still thought she could win, so I better wipe away these tears and get back in the game, right alongside her, every step of the way. This was a race against time; it would need to be a team effort to win.

As the night drew on, word continued to spread far and beyond my scope of realization, more and more people were joining the fight for Kassie's survival through prayer.

*****

I have always been an out-of-the-box thinker and generally never enjoyed conforming to the day-to-day thought processes that most were perfectly content with. I would begin laying the groundwork for everyone working with Kassie at PCH to believe Kassie could survive the night, but I needed accurate information first. I started probing the doctors with questions.

I asked, "In detail, what is the problem that is keeping Kassie from getting better?" I learned that the severity of damage to Kassie's lungs was keeping her from absorbing enough oxygen to be delivered through her blood to the vital organs that keep her alive. When this happens to the body, the least important organs shut down one at a time in order to protect the most important organs, the brain and heart.

I asked, "Can we do a lung transplant so Kassie could do what was necessary to get better?" I was told that was not a technologically viable option, nor would time allow.

I asked, "Why don't we do a blood transfusion and give Kassie new blood?" I was told that would not be effective because the problem was not the blood, but the fact that oxygen could not get into the blood through the lungs.

I continued peppering them with a litany of dead-end questions, hoping upon hope that there was something a layman could come up with that a trained specialist in children's medicine hadn't yet.

I then decided to start stacking the deck with the people who were working with Kassie. They needed to know Kassie. They needed to know it was Kassie lying there in the bed fighting for her life. She had a brother and a sister and knew how to win a tractor race. They needed to be made aware that she was a drama queen and an outstanding athlete, and that she was going to be a princess when she grew up. I could tell it was uncomfortable for them to talk with me. I understood that not getting too close to patients and families was probably a good defense mechanism. But they talked with me anyway and were very courteous and professional. Of course, they told me they would do everything possible, but I still went around to each and every person to speak with them personally one by one. They had to understand that Kassie would refuse to be an unnamed statistic regarding this strep pneumococcal pneumonia that was ravaging her lungs and body; they had to understand that Kassie always found a way to do something that nobody else could do. I promised that Kassie wasn't their typical patient. I explained Kassie's philosophy of her glass always being three-fourths full. I explained that she was an athlete, and she was in perfect condition to fight. I told them of her competitiveness and her spirit. I told them about her ability to be a winner against all odds. Then, after making sure I had their eye contact, I said, "Please don't give up on Kassie, because she doesn't know the meaning of stop, and she won't give up on herself. Please don't you give up on her, please." That drew long looks into my eyes from each person I spoke with that night, without exception. They saw the pain in my eyes, the unspoken silent pleading for a miracle. They saw the pain of a daddy not wanting to lose a child. But they also saw the truth of my statement, and my conviction that all was not lost. Kassie's race could still be won.

Each and every one of the doctors and nurses now had a greater understanding of Kassie, the person, the kid, the athlete, the winner, and they were now unafraid to look into our eyes as they passed in and out of the room. They now had a personal stake in Kassie's outcome and were openly connected. The mood was different than before. They liked Kassie. They felt like they knew her, even though they had only seen her outer shell. They felt they now knew who the real Kassie was inside that shell; the fun, full of life, competitive, frilly dress wearing, cleat toting, dramatic kid who had a beautiful contagious smile and that you couldn't help but love. The kid who knew all too well that "Life's Not Fair," but who would never agree to let that rule win without a huge fight and try to somehow find a way to conquer the challenge.

*****

Late that night, Dr. Tellez approached Lorrie and me privately to talk about something he and his associates had been discussing—a possible emergency treatment for Kassie. He said to us, "Kassie has very little time left. Truth be told, medically, we don't know how she is still alive. What we do know is that she is getting weaker and weaker by the second, as you can tell by the frequency of the alarms going off in Kassie's room." He then said, "If Kassie can survive the night, we have decided that we may be able to do something using very heroic efforts to help save Kassie's life. It's called ECMO, extracorporeal membrane oxygenation." He expressed that this effort would not be without complications, and that it had never actually been attempted with a patient of Kassie's age and size before to his knowledge and for certain not at Phoenix Children's Hospital. He then proceeded to explain what ECMO would entail, and that if we agreed, there would be a heart surgeon available in the morning willing to try the procedure.

First of all, the heart surgeon would place two large cannulae into Kassie, which are like intravenous catheters. One would be into her jugular vein in her neck, and one would be into her femoral vein in her leg. He said honestly that there would be less than a 50 percent chance that Kassie would even be able to survive that initial procedure. If the cannulae placement was successful, Kassie would likely require ECMO for ten days. He said they would have to put Kassie in a medically induced coma to keep her from moving, because if the cannulae were to dislodge, there could be fatal bleeding. If that were to happen, Kassie would bleed out, and it would be very difficult if not impossible to stop. It would be over quickly.

ECMO is something that is usually only done with premature babies. However, Dr. Tellez was recently at a national medical conference where it was discussed that ECMO could possibly be used on older children and adults. The ECMO machine takes the blood from the body, removes the carbon dioxide, adds oxygen, reheats the blood, then pumps the oxygenated blood back into the body. This process circumvents the patient's lungs while a ventilator keeps them inflated, allowing the lungs to continue to mature and form. In Kassie's situation, it would all act exactly the same, except the ventilator would be in place to keep the lungs inflated and allow them to heal.

Dr. Tellez then reiterated the fact that this had never been attempted at PCH with a person of Kassie's size and age, and they would have to improvise an artificial lung large enough for Kassie. He said they were willing to try because of Kassie's strong will and athletic fitness, but that it was up to us whether or not we even wanted to try. In truth, this was well beyond their normal procedures to preserve the patient's dignity and only being offered to us as a last resort effort. He explained that even if all went according to plan, the chances Kassie would ultimately survive were still well below 50 percent.

"With that being said," Dr. Tellez continued, "I do feel that Kassie is a good candidate for this procedure. Even though this is out of the box thinking, it's sound medical theory."

I thought, *A Hail Mary pass into the end zone with no time on the clock in order to tie the game up and get to overtime; giving us a chance to win.*

I asked if there were any other options, to which he replied no.

We asked that if by doing this procedure, Kassie would be put through any additional pain and suffering.

Dr. Tellez explained that Kassie's not the only one who could experience some pain and suffering, but we could also. He cautioned us that should Kassie survive the surgery and make it through ECMO, only to die in the end anyway, they could minimize Kassie's pain and suffering but could not treat ours. The rest of the family would have plenty of anguish due to the prolonged time and the dashed hopes that would ensue. He again reaffirmed that even if the procedure were to be a success, the odds were not in her favor. He said he hated having to say that again, but it was the truth, and what they were suggesting entailed truly heroic efforts. And unfortunately, heroic efforts usually just don't pan out to a happy ending. Further, Kassie had gone a very long time with very little oxygen to the brain. Her oxygen saturation levels, or sat levels as they called them, were in the sixties when she first arrived. The doctors could not determine what effects that would ultimately have on her.

Lorrie and I confirmed we understood what "heroic" meant, and although all efforts may prove to be futile, we felt we had to give Kassie every opportunity to survive. Even if there was only a glimmer of hope, we owed it to Kassie to try. If it did prove to be futile, we would have to deal with our pain, but through that pain, if what they learned while trying to save Kassie resulted in another person's child living at some later time, then Kassie's death would not be in vain.

We signed off on the necessary documentation, and Dr. Tellez went to call the heart surgeon. The heart surgeon had an early morning emergency surgery but was to come and do Kassie's surgery by 8:00 a.m.

As we explained to all of our family and friends what Dr. Tellez was going to try, my sister-in-law, Carroll, exclaimed that she had heard me suggest that earlier in the evening, and they said it couldn't be done.

I said I thought I had suggested it as well, but apparently this was something similar they thought might just work. Either way, it didn't matter to me who came up with the idea as long as they were willing to try something to save my little Kassie.

It was now after midnight. None of our family and friends who had started showing up earlier that night had left. We decided to have Autam and Stevo come to the hospital and felt their need to be with their sister outweighed the distress it would cause them to see her in her current state.

Dr. Lax also went well beyond the call of duty. She was still there when the morning crew began to arrive, even though the final shift of her final day at PCH had ended yesterday. Tomorrow, she would be working at a different hospital, but right now she was doing everything possible for our family. Kassie was her final patient at PCH, and neither Kassie nor Dr. Lax were going down without a fight. Dr. Lax said she would stay all night if necessary, and when the morning shift began arriving, there she was, true to her word.

HEROIC EFFORTS

There was obvious, albeit tempered, excitement from the returning staff that Kassie had survived the night. As the shift change was proceeding, the night shift told the day shift about all the conversations that had gone on; about the heroic procedure that was to be performed, and all they had learned about Kassie and what a fighter she was. There was a new breath of air in their hearts, and many traded in their solemn faces for smiles. Nobody could explain how Kassie could possibly be hanging on, but everyone was very happy she had done it.

Again, the minutes seemed to be hours, and it was excruciating to watch Kassie labor and fight to stay alive. We were all unwitting bystanders, and all we could do was give encouragement, pulling out of Kassie every last ounce of energy and persistence she had to give. She had to hang on a little bit longer, just a little bit longer, just a little bit longer and the heart surgeon would be there. The heart surgeon could give Kassie a chance.

I said out loud, "Kassie, don't give up. You're close to having your surgery done, and the surgery will make it easier for you to win. You're going to get to do something nobody else has done before, but you have to hold on a little bit longer. I know you're tired, but you need to dig deep and gut it out. The surgeon's almost here to help you."

I pictured all the times in Kassie's short life that I had done this same type of thing from the sidelines, or the coach's box, or from the stands. How many times had Kassie heard my words, given me a nod, and met the challenge? How many times had she heard her coaches shout encouragement and done what was asked of her? Could she respond to my words one more time?

I repeated, "Kassie! This is your daddy! Listen to me! Don't give up! You're close to having your surgery done, the surgery that will make it easier for you to win. You're going to get to do something nobody else has done before, but you have to hold on a little bit longer! I'm telling you to hold on a little bit longer. I know you're tired, but you need to dig deep and gut it out, the surgeon's almost here to help you. I "Daddy-Promise" the surgeon will be here at 8:00 a.m., and he will help you to win."

The eight o'clock hour was nearing, and Kassie was miraculously barely hanging on. With each minute came the realization that Kassie may not see the next minute. How was she doing it, how was she able to gut it out? I kept telling her the time and how little amount of time there was until the surgeon arrived. I kept saying, "You can do it! Just a little bit longer, sweetheart, not much longer now. You're doing so good. Everyone is so impressed with how well you are doing. It won't be long now, sweetheart. The surgeon's almost here. Keep fighting, honey. I know you're tired, but Daddy's here to help. Don't give up, baby, the surgeon's almost here."

Word came shortly before 8:00 a.m. that the heart surgeon was delayed with complications on his early morning patient. He was at St. Joe's Hospital and that was only a few minutes away, but he couldn't leave yet. Kassie would need to hold on a bit longer. I looked at them bewildered…how could they do this? They said the doctor would be there at 8:00 a.m. to do the surgery if Kassie could last that long. Kassie did her part. She was still there, fighting and clawing and scratching with every labored breath she took. Kassie did her job, and we've told her it's almost 8:00 a.m. She's using all her strength to last until 8:00 a.m. Damn it, Kassie did her job, and I did my job! This isn't fair!

There was that voice again, but this time it was very prominent. "Life's Not Fair." Kassie hates that rule, AND SO DO I!

I had to focus; I had to compose myself. I had to motivate Kassie to continue fighting. How the hell was I going to do that? I "daddy-promised" her the surgeon would be there at 8:00 a.m.

I stormed into Kassie's room and exclaimed for all to hear that "Life's Not Fair," and told Kassie that we were going into overtime, and the game's on the line. There was no time to be tired, no time to feel sorry for ourselves, there's only time to show these people what Kassie Arner is made of. We don't care if "Life's Not Fair." We're going to hold on until the doctor gets here. I then began speaking to Kassie in a direct manner, not soft and encouraging, but direct and demanding. This took a number of people by surprise, and I kept it up until the heart surgeon arrived. Kassie was trying, but she had reached the end of her reserves, and all the monitors were going off. She was failing, and her oxygen levels were plummeting as word came that the surgeon was in the elevator coming up.

The much-needed heart surgeon was there, and a room in ICU had already been prepped with a full complement of nurses and assistants waiting at the doctor's beck and call. Dr. Teodori briefly introduced himself to Lorrie and me, then hastily went into the room, which had been converted into a temporary operating room. We could hear the doctor barking out instructions like a drill sergeant getting everything just right and telling people that there was not enough time to be messing around. He needed things done, and he needed them done now. The doctor worked with unbelievable precision and speed, while Lorrie and I held each other's hand and talked to everyone about how proud we were of Kassie that she continued fighting until the surgeon got there. Then almost as quickly as it started, it was over. Lorrie and I met with Dr. Teodori, then returned to face our friends and family that were still there. We were in tears, both of us emotionally and physically drained. It was now time to tell everyone what had just happened.

*****

After a phone call to the school, Stevo was very excited to hear that Kassie had gone from a 5 percent chance of living to now having close to a 50 percent chance. He was just learning about percentages in school, so he knew what a huge difference there was between 5 percent and 50 percent. Autam said she had never been so happy about a 50 percent chance but also realized those were the same odds as the flip of a coin. It would be quite a long shot for Kassie to actually survive the ten days that she would be on ECMO. Even though it was miraculous that Kassie survived the night, it would truly take a miracle to bring her through these untested heroic efforts that Dr. Tellez and PCH had come up with.

Kassie was barely out of surgery, and the first of many hurdles had already arrived. As they were getting Kassie attached to the ECMO machine and preparing her to be on the ventilator, there was already a problem.

Dr. Tellez explained, "Try to imagine Kassie's lungs as they try to inflate. Oxygen from the ventilator, or 'vent,' passes through the tube that goes down Kassie's throat. It splits, and one tube goes into the left lung and one tube goes into the right lung. Because Kassie's lungs have sustained such extensive damage, with her left lung worse than the right, her lungs can't inflate. One lung is like leather, the other is like burlap. What it would take to inflate the better lung wouldn't even begin to inflate the worse lung, and to inflate the worse lung would cause the better lung to explode." The doctor continued, "We're going to have to try something that theoretically could work, but I need to let you know that it may not. If it doesn't, there is nothing else we can do for Kassie. Just doing ECMO won't help. Kassie has to have the ventilator, too, for her lungs to get well."

I remember looking up at the ceiling, thinking to myself, "Man, could we not even have five minutes to relish the good news of Kassie surviving the surgery?" I looked to Dr. Tellez to tell us what they were going to try.

He explained they were going to try hooking two vents together, one for each lung. Theoretically, they could communicate with each other, but the reality of the situation was that they were attempting something very technically complicated, and it may not prove to be effective at all. They were wheeling the second vent into Kassie's room, and all we could do was sit and hope.

Kassie's chest was barely moving with each ventilated breath that was pushed into her little body. Then they clicked on the second vent, and the left and right sides of Kassie's chest began rising and falling as the ventilators communicated with each other. First the left, then the right. How strange it was to see each side of Kassie's chest rise and fall at different speeds. We had success! The vents were working in tandem, and Kassie's lungs were expanding and contracting. Again, we could breathe a small sigh of relief. *Two separate vents working together, who would have thought about that*, I wondered. Each of the vents had their own brightly colored letter placed on them; L for left, R for right.

Kassie's bed was put on stilts so there would be enough gravity for the blood to naturally drain to the ECMO machine from the femoral vein before being reoxygenated, warmed, and pumped back into her jugular vein. It was quite a sight, and Kassie's room was quickly filling up with machinery and equipment. The room looked more like a storage room for medical equipment than it did a hospital room.

Elation for Kassie's success was short-lived and soon gave way to another life-threatening problem. The ECMO team was having trouble with the artificial lung. They had calculated the weight of a baby compared to Kassie and multiplied the quantities out, but Kassie still wasn't getting enough oxygen. Her oxygen levels were extremely low, and they were starting to lose her again. Monitor alarms were screaming all over the room. The team feverishly tried to recalculate the estimated lung size and flow, but they were shooting into the dark with no baseline to help them judge accurate measurements. Kassie had spent all the previous day and night fighting for her life, and less than a half hour after going on ECMO, she was already fighting for her life a second time today, and it wasn't even noon yet. I began to wonder if I would be able to take ten days of this.

Although Dr. Tellez had explained this was a really long shot, I didn't fully grasp what a rollercoaster ride this was to be, and that life was not like it was in the movies where there was a miraculous operation, and everything was immediately all right. I was continually getting jolted with bursts of adrenaline. I felt as if I hadn't slept in days, even though it had actually only been about twenty-six hours. With life and death hanging in the balance and the ECMO team trying to get things sorted out, Kassie was still somehow holding onto her precious life. Through all this adversity, Kassie was still fighting. Finally, her oxygen sats began to rise. The ECMO team had been multiplying their calculations by tens but realized they needed to be multiplying by hundreds to get Kassie the oxygen she needed. Apparently, going from baby's weight to people's weight requires more than a one-to-one ratio in calculations. Thank goodness, somebody on that team thought outside the box or Kassie would have been lost right then and there. Now we had to wait and see how Kassie's body would react to being on 100 percent life support while in a medically induced coma. Everybody involved was in totally uncharted territory and would have to think on their feet as things came up.

The new first order of business was to build two sets of steps so the nurses could get up high enough and take care of Kassie. She was literally five feet up in the air due to the stilts being used for ECMO, and I don't think one of her nurses was much more than a smidge above five feet tall. They were standing on chairs, or anything else they could find, until the steps arrived. They commissioned the job to be done by the maintenance department. Somebody must have had some woodshop classes in their past, because in no time at all, two sets of three-step stairs arrived. They were about five feet long, so up to six people could stand on them at the same time, three per side. One set was put on each side of the bed, and they were solid as a rock. There was no rocking when you stood on them, and even though they were put together quickly, they were built to last. I thought, *Our guys at Shea Homes couldn't have done any better of a job.*

*****

It was now Thursday and word had barely broken about Kassie's dire situation when the first stuffed animal arrived that morning via special courier from my coworker Tom Horiza, one of Shea Homes's most talented sales agents. I had been in communication with my work partner, Dottie Hagan, and she was passing the info along via email to Shea company-wide. My managers, Buddy Satterfield and Bob Crandall, were exceptional and told me to take any time necessary while Kassie was fighting for her life, and that everything would be handled for me at work. I told them I would try to make it in for the sales meeting Friday morning to give everyone an update on what was going on. Buddy and Bob said they didn't feel that was necessary, and that I should stay here to be with Kassie. After much deliberation, I agreed that would be the best course of action. I had to settle for the knowledge that my most sincere thank-you would have to be delivered by email to everyone who was pulling for Kassie at work.

Lorrie and I began asking questions regarding if Kassie's illness could be spread to us, Kassie's siblings, or her friends. Word had spread through Kassie's school and some of the parents of Kassie's best friends were concerned for the health of their children. Nobody had ever heard of strep pneumonia. Was it contagious? Was there an inoculation that could be administered? How do you catch it? As a parent, while you certainly have concern for someone else's children, the health of your own kids is always paramount. We began making phone calls to people and giving them accurate info about what was going on. We all went down to our family doctor's office and got a preventative shot just to make sure, as did some of Kassie's closest friends.

While we were getting our shots, I asked our doctor, Don, why Kassie got this but somehow the rest of our family didn't. He explained that bacteria strains are very diverse; he likened them to two ten-year-old boys, where one can be very passive and the other extremely aggressive. We all have a form of this airborne bacteria floating around in our nasal passages, but Kassie had a particularly bad, aggressive strain. Kassie also happened to be dilapidated because she had the flu, and this aggressive bacteria grabbed ahold of her and hid behind her flu symptoms, so we didn't know she had it. In Kassie's weakened state, she couldn't fight it off like she normally would, and it made her very sick.

After we got our shots, we went home to shower and change clothes. Lorrie's mom was flying in from Hawaii to take care of the household, while Lorrie and I stayed at the hospital at Kassie's side. Plans were being put into motion for the long haul and our busy, hectic, multifaceted, wonderfully complicated lives came to a screeching halt. There was one job to do—get Kassie well while keeping Autam and Stevo's lives on as normal of a course as possible.

We decided to meet with our neighbors. Kids and parents had been collecting outside our house since we had gotten home. It was time to speak with the parents of our children's friends. It was an unbearable thought to explain all that had happened in such a short amount of time, but they were there to find out what they could do to help, and we wanted them to know what was actually happening instead of hearing things secondhand and third-hand. We decided to have just the adults over at 5:00 p.m. This gave us a little time to shower and change and eat. They could then tell their kids what was going on and save us that drama. Plus, I could only imagine how it would look to the kids to see us all emotional, and I didn't want to scare them more than they already were. When we met with the adults, Lorrie and I ran through the scenario of what was taking place. We told them more than we would have said to the kids waiting outside. We decided that it would be best to keep their kids less informed than the entire truth and left it up to the parents to relay the info to their kids. We had to explain to them that while Kassie had survived the surgery, there was still less than 50 percent odds that Kassie would survive the ten days of ECMO treatments; and that even if she did survive, we don't know what effect the lack of oxygen had to her brain. It was all so surreal, and I had trouble talking while I choked back the tears. I was taken aback by the genuine concern they had, not just for Kassie, Lorrie, and me, but for that of Autam and Stevo as well. They all offered to have the kids stay at their houses and said they could rotate as long as necessary until things leveled out for us, and until Lorrie's mom, Caren, arrived. Though Autam and Stevo would be staying with my parents during the interim, Lorrie and I still felt very lucky to have such wonderful neighbors and friends. Stevo and Kassie went to the same school, and I knew I would have to go down sooner or later to fill in the administration regarding what was happening, but that would be another day. For now, it was back to the hospital to be with Kassie.

*****

When we arrived at the hospital, there were a lot of people in Kassie's room. They were in the middle of shift change, and all the ICU doctors were conversing about her prognosis. They were taking X-rays of Kassie's chest to see how her lungs were withstanding the merciless onslaught of the strep pneumo bacterial infection. It was still way too early to tell if these heroic efforts were going to have any effect, or if it was just too little too late for Kassie.

After the doctors finished their rounds and got up to speed on all their patients' current conditions, things slowed down a bit. I found that late in the evening, the doctors, nurses, and techs had more time to talk with you. There was finally time to connect with everyone on a one-on-one basis; to get to know them as a person, whether they had kids or not, if they were married and for how long, what their hobbies were. The personal things you find out from a new friend once you're able to spend some time with them.

Many family members would stay with Kassie until late in the evening, and then many would return in the mornings, others in the afternoon or evening once they got off work. My brother Steve would stay very late and then bring large assortments of muffins and pastries for the PCH staff very early in the morning on his way to work. Kassie seemed to always have a room full of visitors both earlier and later than most patients. The staff at PCH began to tell us there was something different about Kassie's room; something they felt when they entered, and it was something they had never witnessed before. They told us they felt good when they were in her room, like there was a positive presence. Many of them were trading shifts so they would be able to work in Kassie's room. It seemed to me like they were being drawn toward her and wanted to make sure everything that could be done would be done.

Lorrie and I decided the best way for us to be productive was to stay at the hospital for thirty-six hours at a time. Each of us could be gone for six to eight hours to go home and rest or to see the kids, and we would still be together for over twenty-four hours at the hospital. Even when one of us was out, there were always others there at the hospital to keep us company or to spell us while we went to the cafeteria. My sister Saundra was there continuously it seemed. She and her husband Coy had just been through a very traumatic event with their nephew in Nevada. He had died in a car accident shortly before Kassie got sick. Saundra confided in me while we were together at Kassie's bedside that she didn't know if she could take any more and that she was about at the end of her rope. Still, there she was at Kassie's bedside stroking Kassie's arm, brushing her hair, and talking with her about what a trooper she was. She kept telling Kassie that everyone was so proud of her, how much the doctors and nurses liked her, and that she had so many good friends asking about her. Aunt Saunie also told Kassie what was going on with her sons, Travis and Casey, which were Kassie's cousins. Best of all, Aunt Saunie let Kassie know what new Beanie Baby was sitting on her shoulder. Saunie worked for a florist and had bought Kassie each individual Beanie Baby character that was released for sale, and they sat vigilantly on patrol; on Kassie, her bed, and the surrounding area. Sometimes, we even put them to work, sitting them in Kassie's hand so she would be able to feel their love.

By midway through the second day, the ECMO team had pretty much worked out all the bugs in the system, and they acted much more relaxed now compared to those first moments just a day earlier. There were three shifts a day, so there was someone sitting at the ECMO machine twenty-four hours a day; they never left Kassie's bedside and were to be there for the entire ten days. We learned that having Kassie on ECMO for longer than ten days would really open the door to infection and other complications resulting in fatal sepsis, so no matter what, this was all that could be done. The team constantly monitored Kassie's vitals and made sure the cannulae were holding in place. If they began seeping blood, which was a definite possibility because of the blood thinners she was on, there would be nothing they could do to stop the bleeding, so it was direly important that Kassie not move for the entire ten days she was being treated on ECMO. Of course, this created some problems because Kassie had to be moved some to keep bedsores from forming. They had Kassie wear special foamy cushions on her feet to keep her heels from getting sores and also to keep her Achilles tendons from being damaged. Kassie was still in need of constant nursing, and the alarms sounded all too frequently.

On the third day, Kassie developed a low-grade fever, and her oxygen sats were not doing well. Autam was there giving Kassie goals to shoot for. She knew that Kassie loved getting rewards, so every time Kassie improved and accomplished what Autam had set for her, she got a little something tucked into the plush Elmo backpack hanging next to the hospital bed. Maybe it was a piece of candy for an uptick on her oxygen sats or one of Autam's nail polishes that Kassie always used to sneak from Autam's room and use. Autam used whatever she could come up with that she felt would motivate her little sister. Even now, Kassie's big sister was coaching her to not give up.

Kassie's pulmonologist, Dr. Gong, came in and checked how Kassie's lungs were sounding. I sat on the far end of the room under the window that Lorrie's sister, Debbie, had painted for Kassie, with her infamous dove in flight as well as the inscription, "Hi, I'm Kassie! Room 407." After the doctor finished examining her, he came over and we talked for a little while. I had already told him Kassie was a good little athlete. I was curious about the damage to her lungs and if that would hinder her from competing at more competitive levels later on. Mind you, we didn't even know if Kassie was going to survive for five more minutes, but I felt I needed to know that if she were to survive, whether she would be able to do the things she loves to do.

Dr. Gong said that the damage to her lungs was severe and that at Kassie's age, the body stops producing new lung tissue. However, he reassured me that even though she may not be able to be an Olympic-class athlete, she would still be able to compete.

I was very happy to hear this, even though I didn't listen to that little voice in my head telling me he probably just said that to make me feel better about things; I knew that Kassie ever walking out of this hospital was a long shot at best. We talked a little longer, and I told him some of my favorite stories about Kassie and her athletics, then he had to go but said he would be back the following day.

*****

I went down to the cafeteria for about fifteen minutes. As I got back up to Kassie's floor, I saw a bunch of people running into her room. I could see and hear all of Kassie's monitors sounding. We were all standing around Kassie's bed, while the doctors and nurses worked feverishly to get Kassie's vitals under control; she was crashing, and her temperature was rising, 103 degrees, 104 degrees, 105 degrees. There was so much medical equipment and machines in her room that it was hard not to be in the way. All we could do was tell Kassie to keep fighting, don't give up, we know it's hard and you're tired, but you can't stop fighting right now. I told Kassie that I loved her and for her to please keep fighting. We had been receiving cards and letters from all over, from family and friends, and people we didn't know who had heard about Kassie. She had multitudes of stuffed animals and balloons, so many things that we had actually started taping them to the walls so everyone who came into Kassie's room could read all the cards and letters. I was looking at the doctor trying to figure out what could be done when he looked up at me, the nurses were looking to him as well and saw the look, too. He looked at me with a frown on his face and shook his head slightly, his eyes full of compassion. Kassie was crashing; her body was beginning to reject the lifesaving measures that were being administered to keep her alive. I stood there on autopilot saying words of encouragement while my mind raced. This was it; I was losing my little girl, and there was nothing anyone in that room could do about it. I continued telling Kassie she had to keep fighting and that Daddy was here to help her. I repeated over and over, "Just keep on going, baby, keep on going."

Everyone was silent with their heads down and their eyes closed. Some were holding hands, and I heard weeping. Kassie's valiant fight was over. She had done everything that was asked of her for so long, but the infection was just too advanced for her to overcome the odds. I was dead inside, and I looked down at Kassie's lifeless body in disbelief. There was nothing left except the alarms from all the equipment going off at the same time.

Right then, the nurse standing closest to me started reading a card out loud that was hanging on the wall next to Kassie's bed that my aunt had sent from Oklahoma. Before she started, the nurse said, "Lord, if there was ever a time to listen, it is now." She began reading the card.

"The Lord has a plan for all of us, and watches over and loves all of his children." Then she read the handwritten part. "I pray that His plan for you is a full quick recovery and that you fulfill His purpose for you."

As soon as she finished, the alarms began to quiet one at a time, and her temperature began dropping to near 100 degrees. Her vitals went back to being fairly normal, and everyone around the bed was totally dumbfounded.

Someone leaned over to me and whispered, "Many said Kassie surviving that first night was a miracle. I've never actually witnessed a miracle before, but I'm pretty sure we just saw one."

I went to the corner of the room with my back to everyone and just wept. Lorrie came over and squeezed me tight. The nurses then all gathered around to comfort us. I turned around to thank them. Their faces showed that nothing needed to be said, and not a word was spoken by anyone. I hugged each of them one at a time while continuing to weep. I was emotionally drained, and I collapsed down into a chair trying to fathom what I had just witnessed.

ECMO Machine

Dad reading to Kassie

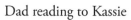

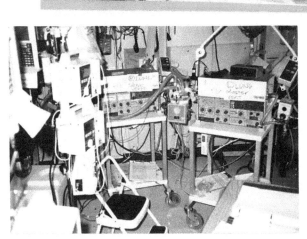

Artificial Lungs L and R

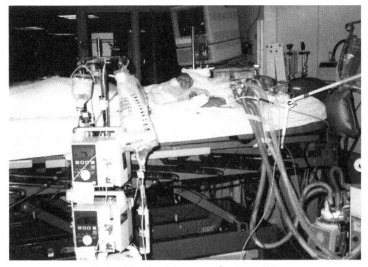

Raised bed with stairs for ECMO

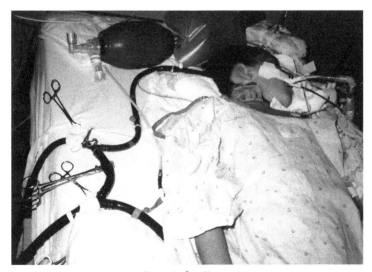

Circuit for Ecmo

PCH ECMO nurses Jill and Alicia

After that, we had a steady stream of well-wishers who visited the room. Some were hospital staff members from different floors of the hospital who had heard about what happened, others were patients and their loved ones who had overheard people talking. Many would casually walk by Kassie's room and peer in, but few were able to continue their casual pass by without stopping and gazing at the sheer magnitude of the undertaking that was Kassie's room. Most would ultimately strike up a conversation, wanting our permission to come in and see the "Miracle Girl on the 4th Floor." Word had definitely spread throughout the hospital about Kassie. As it would do no harm, I felt compelled to share our miracle. We allowed any and all to come in and pray next to Kassie. I was so thankful that God was intervening with Kassie, but at the same time, I was feeling ashamed that He was doing so despite my unworthiness; I was having issues dealing with it internally. It was late in the evening, and Dr. Tellez came in and asked me if I would like to join him in the doctor's lounge.

As we got to the lounge and sat down, Dr. Tellez asked me how I was doing. I confided to him my most inner feelings. I told him that I felt I was very unworthy to ask God for anything, and that it would be hypocritical for me to do so. Dr. Tellez sat and listened to me without interruption, then gave me a pamphlet containing Bible verses. He began talking to me about the power of God. I thought, *A doctor talking to me about the power of God?*

He said to me in no uncertain terms that there is absolutely no medical reason whatsoever that Kassie should still be alive. He told me that he is a firm believer in the power of God and how he is able to do things with his hands at times that are way beyond his own capabilities.

He also explained that only God knows Kassie's outcome, and it has already been determined. We are just playing things out like actors in a big play. All we can do is our best and trust Him for the outcome. He continued, "Kassie living or dying is totally out of our hands, and it's out of yours as well." He then told me, "If you really feel the way you have said, it is really very simple to fix your problem. Just ask for Jesus to come into your heart, open the door, and let Him in."

For some reason, the knowledge that Kassie's outcome had already been decided brought me a serene comfort; I don't know why, it just did. Maybe it was because it gave me hope that what I was doing in my own small way to motivate Kassie was similar to how Dr. Tellez could do things as a doctor that were above his abilities. Even if the outcome was decided, the actions that we choose to take could be a part of the reason that Kassie could survive. To sit back and passively allow things to happen could change the outcome that had already been determined. All of sudden, I felt like I was in a quantum physics class. That certainly gave me a lot to consider, but I was thankful that Dr. Tellez had taken the time to help me through my self-imposed roadblock, and with his help, I asked Jesus Christ into my life right there in the doctor's lounge. It was strange because I didn't feel like I "had" to do it for Kassie's situation; I wanted to do it for myself. I didn't feel hypocritical like I thought I would, or as if the reason I was asking Christ into my life was for some ulterior motive to benefit myself or Kassie, like I had pictured it many times before. I knew there was a very small chance that Kassie would survive, but I had renewed vigor to listen to that little voice in my head for any clues to enable me to help in any way I could.

*****

On the fourth day that Kassie was at PCH, they finally allowed Stevo to come and see his sister. Actually, truth be told, they snuck him in. Due to his age and the time of the year that it was, they were keeping younger kids out of the Critical Care area because of some seasonal germs that were going around in his age bracket. With Stevo being nine years old, he really didn't have a good concept of life and death; but he definitely had a grasp on how his mommy and daddy were reacting to the situation, and how his teachers, friends, and his friends' parents were talking with him. Everyone wanted to know how he was doing and asking him for any new info about his sister.

While Stevo was visiting that afternoon, there was a steady stream of doctors and nurses filtering in and out of the room. Stevo was continually being asked to scoot one way or the other off the steps from either side of the bed. At one point, there were so many people standing around Kassie's bedside administering care that he had to go and sit in the chair by the window.

While we were sitting there together, I was catching up on what all was going on with him and asking how he was doing at school.

He said that everyone is being really nice to him, and he was getting a lot of attention from people he didn't even know, asking him questions about Kassie that he didn't know how to answer, and it made him feel bad that he didn't know what to say or do.

I told him it was okay to tell people that he didn't know what the answer was, and that if people had questions, they could talk with his teacher, the principal, or Kassie's teacher. I explained how important it was to allow people to know what was going on, because there were a lot of people thinking about Kassie and wishing for her to be well soon. I told him that some are even praying for her to get well, and they need to be assured that their prayers are being heard and are helping. I told him that we needed everyone to keep praying for Kassie's recovery and it's okay to let people know that.

He continued, "I'm praying for her, too, and Grama Nelson says our prayer with us at bedtime." He then recited "our prayer that we say together at bedtime."

"God Bless Mommy and Daddy, and Autam and Kassie and Steve, and Splash and Annie and Wiggles, and Grandmas and Grandpas, and Aunts and Uncles and Cousins and Nephews, and God Bless America and everyone in it, and God Bless me…" then he exclaimed, "and we added…and God, please pay special attention to Kassie, she really needs your help right now, and help her to get well and come home soon. Amen."

I told him I thought that new part at the end was great, and I am sure that will help Kassie get better quicker.

He was quiet for a little bit, then looked up at me and asked, "Daddy, is Kassie going to die and live in heaven? I know heaven is a good place to be, but I don't want Kassie to go there. I want her to come home. I want her to wake up and come home."

I began to tear up, and I couldn't respond to him right away, so I just kinda looked at him and tried to smile while I attempted to compose myself.

I have been told that what makes great sales agents is their ability to empathize so well with people. However, one of the drawbacks to *my* empathy is that I am also extremely sensitive to other's situations, and I can't seem to do anything other than wear those emotions on my sleeve for everyone to see. I so envy my brother Steve; he is able to keep his emotions in check and function normally. I always felt there was a standard that men are held up to, and showing emotion is looked down upon. I never hide my emotions from my kids; that is the way I am, and that is the way it is. However, it does get in the way, just like now, when I needed to be answering Stevo's question and reassuring him, but instead there I sat, having to pull myself together.

Stevo was looking down at his feet when I began responding. I said to him, "Stevo, you know that Kassie's really sick, and there is a chance that she won't be able to survive, but we aren't thinking about that. We are all concentrating and focusing on doing everything necessary to make Kassie better so she can come home. Each minute that Kassie stays alive is one minute more that we have with her, that we can tell her we love her and want her to get well, and that it is important for her to keep fighting to stay alive. Do you understand, son?"

He nodded his response.

I then told him, "Kassie has a team, a very large team that is helping her to fight this battle. All of these doctors and nurses are members of Kassie's team, and we are members of Kassie's team, too."

"And Mommy and Autam?" Stevo excitedly asked.

"Yep, they are, too," I answered. "Just like all of your and Kassie's friends and teachers at school, and all the guys on your baseball team.

They are members of Kassie's team." I asked him if he thought our two dogs, Splash and Annie, and Kassie's bird, Wiggles, would like to be on our team since they love Kassie, too.

Stevo agreed that maybe if he told them how much we needed their help, they could help, too.

I said, "Stevo, look around this room. There isn't one inch of wall space that isn't covered with cards or letters or hand drawn pictures. This is a double room, and as full as it is with all this equipment in here helping to keep Kassie alive, it is just as full of love, also helping to keep Kassie alive. That wall is sixteen feet long at least and ten feet tall, plus the front wall and this wall where the window is, that's a lot of love from a lot of people. All of those people are on Kassie's team. People we don't even know that have been told about how much Kassie needs their prayers are part of Kassie's team. Every one of those people need to know their prayers are being heard, and their prayers are being answered. They need to know that Kassie needs them to continue praying for her because Kassie is still very sick, and we still need their help so Kassie can come home."

He said he understood and then told me that people driving by on the street below could be part of Kassie's team, too.

I asked him how that would work.

He pointed to the window, "See, Dad!"

I looked but still didn't see, and I kind of cocked my head to the side with a puzzled look on my face.

Stevo looked at me and proclaimed, "Right there! It says 'Hi, I'm Kassie! Room 407' and it's written backwards so people can read it from outside."

I had seen that window a hundred times but never got it until my nine-year-old son explained it to me.

I said, "You are absolutely right. I had not noticed that. Now even more people than I thought are on Kassie's team."

With that, we enjoyed the view from Kassie's window that was shaped like a huge porthole on a ship. We admired the flying dove, the Barbie, the ferocious Taz, and the huge blossoming flower painted on Kassie's window; all of whose brilliant colors could draw attention from a mile away. I made a mental note to check to see if you could actually read it from the street as you were driving by four stories below, and amazingly, yes, you could.

*****

Kassie's hospital room 407 window

While we kept Autam and Stevo updated on their sister's condition, we tried to keep their lives going forward with normal activities. Lorrie's mom, Caren, had arrived from Maui the previous day and was settling into everyone's hectic routine.

Lorrie and I decided the best way to get info out to everyone was to leave the most current information on the answering machine message. It would also free up Caren from having to repeat the same info over and over again. That way, anyone wanting to find out how Kassie was doing could just call and listen. They could leave a message for Kassie if they wanted, and we would relay it to her the next time we were at the hospital. I was told by many that they would call, not knowing what to expect from one day to the next, understanding that a call to the answering machine could be excruciating to listen to, or it may be an inspirational message about an accomplishment Kassie had made, or an obstacle she had overcome. Sometimes, it was both excruciating and uplifting. The message would always remind them their prayers were working and how much we appreciated their continued prayers for Kassie.

Caren was instrumental in helping Lorrie and I keep our sanity by completely taking over for us in the everyday activities that had to continue going on, whether we were there or not. She literally stepped in and became the rudder to the "Arner ship," which was a magnanimous task. Our family is very active, and we were always on the go to the kids' practices, games, or any one of a dozen different activities we were involved in. Caren prepared the meals for the family, made and fielded phone calls for us, and passed along appropriate information to the proper people. Without Caren, our lives would have stayed at that screeching halt, and that would not have been good for anyone.

Caren was familiar with adversity and knew how to deal with taking difficult situations and turning them into positive outcomes. Lorrie was the oldest of four daughters, and Caren held the task of raising them primarily on her own. Lorrie's father, Jim, was a high-wire lineman for utility companies across the southwest United States, which kept him on the road a substantial amount of time. Caren was great at making ends meet and made sure that the girls didn't go without, even though that meant she herself went without most of the time.

Caren was a wonderful time manager and made sure our household operated efficiently, while Lorrie and I spent most of the time at the hospital. I was very grateful that she was able to come and help us during our time of need, and she was instrumental in keeping Autam and Stevo on track. They had time to do homework, continue their sports activities, and to visit at the hospital daily. I jested with her that we might just need to keep her around, but I knew she would never leave Maui, where she had made a name and life for herself, and where she relished her independence.

I was also very fortunate that my parents and Lorrie's parents got along so well. There was never any rivalry BS that happens sometimes with families, and my parents told me numerous times how much they enjoyed visiting with Lorrie's parents when they were in town. When we were able to get together for holidays, it was more than congenial, although it was an infrequent happening because Lorrie's parents lived in different states. Caren joked, albeit probably true, that she and Jim got along a lot better and liked each other more now than when they were married. All in all, I felt very lucky to have my mother-in-law here. I also liked the fact that she told Lorrie when we were newly married that she thought I'd make a million dollars someday.

*****

The video of Kassie's trek to Florida for the "Kids Race Against Drugs" Tractor Race Nationals had been making the circuit through the nurse and staff lounges so people could see Kassie in all her glory, having fun and just being Kassie. That video was very well received by all who watched it, and it was a great representation of who Kassie was. People would come in and say they had heard about Kassie and watched her video. It seemed everyone on the staff at PCH was watching it, except for Kassie's doctors. They said they wouldn't watch it until Kassie was out of the woods. Dr. Liu, one of the main doctors working with Kassie, was quite a bit more reserved than Dr. Tellez, at least it seemed that way to us. He definitely didn't see Kassie's outlook with rose-colored glasses. He was very positive about wanting to make Kassie better, but he wouldn't take the step to give us any reason for hope medically. You could tell that he was very dedicated in doing everything possible to allow for a positive outcome, and he was very personable to us, but he held his cards very close to his chest in regard to Kassie's prognosis. I would challenge myself to get Dr. Liu to give any type of a positive outlook. He would never be negative, instead he would just say, "It's still way too early to say. Kassie is still way too sick to make a guess on an outcome, but she is very strong and doing everything possible that she can do to help us. Let's see how things are once she is through ECMO."

Kassie was having three X-rays a day of her chest to see how her lungs were doing. Throughout the four days that Kassie had been at Phoenix Children's Hospital, there had been some improvement, but not enough for anyone to say yet that Kassie might actually survive this. I asked a lot of questions of the doctors and nurses regarding their opinions on situations based on their experience.

I'd ask, "As of right now, what do you feel the chances are of Kassie making it through ten days of ECMO?"

Or I'd ask the ECMO techs, "What do you feel the chances are of having to go the full ten days of treatment, and if we absolutely had to, could we go longer?"

I asked the neurologist, Dr. Bernes, "What do you feel the chances are, because of the oxygen deprivation Kassie suffered, that Kassie will wake up and be the same little girl we knew before she got sick?"

Kassie—
You're making us work - girl!
Dr. "T" Dave Tellez

ARVA BYNUM RN

Paul Lite Intensivist

It seemed like everyone was on the same page, they didn't know. We were all flying blind, because by all intents and purposes, Kassie shouldn't still be alive, but the fact that she was, made those longshot odds incalculable.

I did get an answer to one of my questions though. "Shouldn't we be covering Kassie with an iron apron when you take an X-ray with the portable machine?" That answer was yes. I don't know it for a fact, but I think that everyone knew it was such a stretch for Kassie to survive this, that it just didn't cross anyone's mind to protect the rest of Kassie's body from the X-rays. Even though I was still a basket case in my own mind about the thought of losing my little girl, I outwardly projected that she was going to survive this, and I felt it prudent to make sure that everyone else acted like she would survive, too.

The following day, Dr. Bernes was back in and said he wanted to speak with both Lorrie and me. As we sat down with him, I could tell by his demeanor that this wasn't going to be a fun visit. I felt the best-case scenario was that he was having a bad day…man did I hope he was just having a bad day.

He started off by saying, "I know you are very involved in Kassie's recovery, and you have questions about Kassie's potential outcomes. There is very little accurate info that could provide us with concrete-solid benchmarking regarding her brain because of the medication that was given to Kassie in order to keep her in a coma while the ECMO procedure continues. Given that, I want to prepare you with the potential outcomes as far as how Kassie may emerge from this. That is of course providing she survives the rest of the treatments."

I asked if this was regarding the questions I had been asking over the last few days and he said, "Yes, partially."

He continued by saying, "Your little girl is really quite some-thing. She has already astounded most of us in the medical community by actually surviving this long. You both realize that, don't you? I'm not telling you anything you don't already know, right?"

Lorrie and I both responded that we were very well aware of that, and he hadn't offended us by saying so. We also let him know it was okay to talk to us about the truth of the situation, but we preferred not to discuss anything that could be negative within earshot of Kassie; that we were continuing to push Kassie to still fight for a positive outcome.

He nodded and we moved from Kassie's bedside to the other end of the room, next to Kassie's decorated window. As we walked over, Dr. Bernes couldn't help but notice Kassie's walls were entirely covered with cards and letters and pictures filled with encouragement for Kassie to get better. When we got to the chairs by the window and sat down, Dr. Bernes asked if we had heard that Kassie is being referred to as the Miracle Girl.

We said yes that we were aware and that we had quite a few well-wishers visit Kassie. Many asked if they could come in and see the "Miracle Girl." Some who work at the hospital and others who had heard about her and came to see her room and pray for her as well.

I continued, "We allow them to, and they are always astonished with the amount of equipment that is in the room, and the fact that Kassie's bed is on stilts. Then they hesitantly walk up the steps to see her and say a prayer next to her. We are really quite appreciative that total strangers are willing to try and help our little girl with a personal prayer. It just goes to show you what type of people there are in this world and the type of people that work at this hospital as well."

He nodded his head and said that he felt compelled to talk with us about some of the possibilities of what to expect, should Kassie defy the odds and survive the ten days of treatments. As we sat there intently listening, he said, "As you are aware, Kassie was deprived of oxygen for some period of time, and the human brain can't survive without oxygen for very long without it sustaining damage. How much time and what level of deprivation Kassie's brain endured the lack of oxygen is somewhat unclear, but you need to prepare yourself for the fact that if and when Kassie wakes up, she may not be the same little girl you had before she got sick. Her mental faculties could have been affected."

I had already pondered this subject matter in my own mind and had come to the conclusion that this would be a bridge to cross once it presented itself. Lorrie and I had not spoken too much about this potential situation, and I was unclear about how she might react to this problem, but as usual, she rode the wave and just nodded her head. I supposed she had thought about it already as well herself.

The doctor then added, "However, the human brain is still somewhat of a mystery, and there is nothing currently showing us that Kassie has any type of damage. The medication is masking true brain function. Personally, I will tell you this though, with Kassie doing what she has done already, I'm rooting and hoping Kassie will be fine when all of this is said and done. I just needed you to know the possibilities. She could have the worst-case scenario, she could come through this unscathed, or she might have some issues that are somewhere in between. We will just have to wait and see."

He also let us know, with our permission, they were planning on temporarily reducing the meds that were keeping her in the coma to check and see if she would wake up, and maybe if she could squeeze a finger or move her arms and legs a little. They needed to do everything possible to verify they were giving her the correct dosages so as not to cause any further damage.

I said, "I thought Kassie had to be as still as possible to ensure the cannulae would stay put."

He agreed and said they would make sure she wouldn't move that much, but they felt it imperative to make sure they weren't giving her too much morphine.

Lorrie and I agreed, and I thought, *Well, that went better than I thought it was going to. It was good to hear that someone thinks there is a chance that Kassie can pull through this procedure and still be the same little girl, or at the very least, he said it out loud. Whether he believes it or not could still actually be open to debate.*

The doctor went to Kassie's bedside and checked a few things, touched her arm and stood silently a moment. He then waved to us saying he would visit again in the next day or two, and finally telling us as he left to "stay strong and keep up the good work."

Lorrie and I looked at each other, and I asked her if he had said anything new that she hadn't thought about.

She shook her head no and said she just really had not wanted to think about that yet.

I agreed, but now that the cat was out of the bag, I asked her, "If Kassie does survive and she has irreparable brain damage, what should we consider doing?" I knew what the answer was for me, and I hoped it was the same for Lorrie.

She said, "No matter what, Kassie is still our little girl, and we will do whatever is necessary to make her happy."

I agreed and followed with, "And she will live with us at our home, right?"

Lorrie agreed, and I was happy we were on the same page, and there was no debate necessary.

She then looked at me and said, "But Kassie will show them what that Arner 'stick-to-it-ness' is all about!"

I smiled at her, gave her a hug and a kiss, and thought to myself how lucky I was to have Lorrie at my side.

*****

Lorrie had been receiving phone calls from friends, and I had gotten calls from some of the teachers from Kassie's school wanting to know if we were allowing kids down to see Kassie. We discussed it and decided that we didn't feel it appropriate to have Kassie's friends see her in her current state, and we certainly didn't want to make things worse for any of them. I was afraid it may cause her friends to have bad dreams or cause them despair, and Lorrie didn't want them to see the way Kassie looked hooked up to all the machines. If this was to be Kassie's time, neither of us wanted anyone's final remembrance of Kassie to be anything other than that she was full of energy and life, what a great friend she was, and how much fun she was to be around. We were hopeful that everyone understood and honored our wishes.

Vanessa Haines was visiting as we discussed allowing kids to come and see Kassie. We had become friends through Stevo's baseball team. Her husband, Mike, was one of the coaches and their son, Garrett, was Stevo's best friend. Vanessa happened to work on the twelfth floor of the hospital and was a regular visitor to Kassie's room. She had given us the idea of having Kassie listen to some of her favorite songs through headphones when she brought in a cassette player that had messages from their kids to Kassie. Vanessa suggested maybe the kids from school could also make tapes for Kassie with get well wishes, and said she would be happy to pick them up and bring them to Kassie so she could hear their recorded messages. We all agreed that would be a great idea, and we thanked Vanessa for coming up with such a brilliant compromise.

As we hung out at Kassie's bedside later that same day, we got a huge surprise. Her teacher, Miss Marbaugh, came in to read aloud to her. As the days rolled along, other teachers and staff members from Kassie's school came and read aloud to her daily. They also brought tape recordings of her friends and classmates reading aloud in class. They were all sending Kassie personal messages to listen to, hoping for her to get well soon. Lorrie and I were overwhelmed by this, and we were literally beside ourselves with the raw emotion this produced. We had been trying to make sure our decisions were the correct ones for everyone, so they figured out a way to come and visit Kassie in a way that would be acceptable, via teachers and tape recordings. As Miss Marbaugh sat at the bedside and read to Kassie, I couldn't help but remember back to when I was ten years old and listening to her read to us in class. I guess it's true that the more things change, the more they stay the same.

I was constantly in awe of how people came to our aid. Not because we asked them to, but because they wanted or needed to. Whatever the reason, it was so appreciated. The types of things people were doing for Kassie were things many would only expect family to do. Obviously, it mattered not that Kassie's friends and teachers weren't blood relatives; they were drawn to Kassie just the same. They were showing their love for her. A love that wasn't predicated by whether or not they were family; but rather, a love that was earned through Kassie's actions and interactions, a love that was real, and a concern to make things better, no matter what the personal cost.

The cards and stuffed animals kept rolling in from my Shea family. Salespeople and office staff were calling me to find out if they could come down and visit. We agreed that it would be fine if they wanted to, but I prefaced it with a brief description of what to expect when they got here. I didn't want their visit to cause them any additional concern than what they were already experiencing. It's tough to see a kid in Kassie's shape when you are a parent. It can't help but get under your skin and into your brain, but still they came, with the full knowledge of what the scene was to be when they arrived.

One thing about working for a large home builder, as well as having lots of friends, is that there are plenty of faiths. There were Catholics, Protestants, Jews, Muslims, Mormons, Jehovah's Witnesses, Baptists, Amish, Lutherans, and I think even a couple of Druids sprinkled in for good measure visiting Kassie. I was constantly reminded about how thoughtful people can be.

Some would come up to us and ask, "We know that we are not the same faith as you and Lorrie, but would it be okay if we were to say a prayer next to Kassie?"

My response was always the same, "I think it would be wonderful if you would take the time to say a prayer for Kassie. We all believe in God, we may call him by a different name and our prayers may go through a different operator, but all calls still go to heaven. Thank you for caring enough about Kassie to be here."

Some people would bring their minister, preacher, or priest with them and ask to pray. My cousin Ronnie even brought in some holy water that had been blessed by their priest to sprinkle over Kassie. It was really inspiring to see how much people actually care. I found myself not only wanting Kassie to survive and be healthy in all ways for myself, but now also for the many others that were going out of their way to do what they could to help Kassie. I started realizing that not only would it devastate our family if we were to lose our little girl, but it would also be traumatic, if not devastating, to other families that had put so much effort forth for Kassie. That gave me even greater inspiration to do and think of anything possible to ensure a positive outcome.

Caren-Grama Nelson and Aunt Debbie

Kassie in forced slumber

Taz blanket

For as well as Kassie was plodding along with her ECMO, she was still way behind in the race against her sworn enemy, the bacteria. It was now becoming a real question whether Kassie's lungs were going to be at a point of healing that would make a difference at the end of the ten days. She was being bombarded with heavy doses of antibiotics and oxygen, and still the bacteria was not subsiding. As hard as Kassie and her entire "team" were fighting to overtake the infection, it was just too prominent in her system for the meds to take over. If there was only something else to do, but what? Nobody knew.

I finally decided to bring in a new coach for Kassie's team. A person who had a huge winning record and who knew how to pull off upset victories. This new coach would be able to direct a huge comeback, and if this person couldn't do it, I knew no other human being that could. Although the new coach was young, I felt in my gut she was ready for the task. On day six of the medical ordeal, Kassie Arner was named as Head Coach of "Team Red and White."

As I stood above Kassie, I proclaimed to all within earshot of her promotion from player to coach and explained what her job entailed. I said, "Kassie, while all of us that are currently on your team out here will continue doing everything necessary that we can, you are now in charge of your team that's inside you. Your team is made up of red and white blood cells. They have to be positioned all over your body for you to win. The red and white blood cells are very smart, and they will do anything they are told to do by you since you're their coach, just like when you followed the orders of your coaches, so will they. They are also very fast, just as fast as you are, and all of their nicknames are 'Speedy,' just like your nickname. So basically, Kassie, you are coaching an entire team of Kassies, just waiting to be told what to do so they can perform and find a way to win, just like you always have, no matter how difficult. Your enemy is 'the Green Team.' They are the mucus and gunk that is in your lungs, and the bacterial infection that is still pulsing through your body trying to kill you. Your goal is to stop the spread of the Green Team and send Team Red and White throughout your body so you can heal yourself and win. The Green Team are huge cheaters, and even though they are slow and aren't very smart, they are very strong, so you can't be overconfident. Your opponents are way ahead and very close to winning, so you need to get your team organized. There is absolutely no time to rest. Your job starts as soon as I give you the final instructions. Okay, Kassie, listen up! This is very important so pay close attention. Your job number one is to have Team Red and White get your oxygen flowing. Now I will explain what you need to do."

I explained where to start, while my brother Steve pressed gently on Kassie's heart and continued applying pressure wherever I was telling her to have her Team Red and White go. "First, you start at your heart and send your team to your lungs, then to your neck and up into your face and into your brain. Then down to your shoulders and all the way down to your elbows, then to your wrists and finally into your fingers, and then all the way back up to your shoulders again. Next, go down your sides and back, into your hips, then your hamstrings and thighs, and down to your knees and into your calves, down to your ankles, and into your feet, and then through each of your toes. From there, go back up to your heart so that the next leg of Team Red and White can deliver oxygen to all the same parts of your body that we just visited."

Then my brother and I would do it again. "Okay, Kassie, pay attention, because this is your job now." As I repeated the instructions, my brother would trace the path she was to take while she coached her team.

My brother sat there for hours, silently tracing that same path on Kassie, while I would let her know to keep vigilant. I told her the Green Team was setting up traps to keep Team Red and White from accomplishing their task, and it was important that she coach her team and tell them what to do. If the Green Team sat up a roadblock so Team Red and White couldn't get through, she had the authority to direct her team around any adversity they may find. I explained to her that because her team was so fast, they would easily be able to get around their enemy by taking a different route. Her team would be through to the next point before the Green Team ever even knew they had been outsmarted and "outquicked" by Team Red and White. I explained that her team of red and white blood cells were so smart and fast, no matter how much the Green Team cheated and tried to trick them, they would never be able to completely stop Team Red and White. The Green Team could not win as long as Kassie was paying attention and coaching her team through the hazards and multiple obstacles that the enemy would throw at them.

I said, "Kassie, once you get the Green Team on the ropes, show no mercy and continue pummeling them and pummeling them until they are defeated. Don't allow them to get a foothold anywhere else in your body. If you see them starting to build a stronghold, send another group of Team Red and White to bust them up. You have a bunch of groups that make up your 'Inside' team, so you don't have to worry about running out of players. Once you get the hang of it, feel free to send Team Red and White throughout your body one group after another. The Green Team is big and strong, but they can't handle the speed of Team Red and White. As you get stronger, send out your team in massive quantities. There is no limit to how many players you can have on the field at one time. Go ahead and show them what Team Red and White can do with Kassie Arner as their coach."

I knew that this sounded desperate, far-fetched, and maybe even futile to some, but I didn't care. That little voice inside my head told me I should get Kassie more involved, and if she became more focused on how she needed to fight for herself, I would provide the best game plan I could for her.

Our friends and family were getting into the spirit of things by bringing in red and white stuff to place on Kassie's already filled walls. There were red and white pompoms. My brother brought in an Oklahoma Sooners football jersey. There were new hand drawn pictures showing Kassie as the coach of Team Red and White. There were hand-made cards made of red paper with white crayon writing. We would tell Kassie every time something new came in that was red and white. I honestly think the staff at PCH thought we had lost our minds, but the next day, those in the know were all wearing red and white scrubs.

In truth, there were some people feeling that I was pushing Kassie too hard, and that I was putting too much pressure on her to perform. A few felt that Kassie should be able to just lay there in the bed and let God and medicine take its course. While no person ever said anything directly to me, I would hear these types of comments from different third parties keeping me abreast on the goings on of the outside world. Since Kassie got to the hospital, I hadn't read a newspaper or watched a newscast. I was in my own little world and didn't have time for distractions. I would listen to the concerns of others and acknowledge them, but I had already been told by numerous physicians and specialists that there was no medical reason why Kassie was still alive. While it was true that all of the medical technology in Kassie's room was helping to keep her alive, it was God and Kassie who had gotten her this far. I also knew in my soul that if we wanted to beat this strep pneumo, we had to get Kassie involved in the outcome. I had asked everyone involved to not give up on Kassie, and I had promised everyone that Kassie wouldn't give up on herself. I meant it, and Kassie was proving it. But just like every great athlete, you have to keep them involved, or they don't perform at their maximum potential. I knew that if Kassie were able to talk right now, she would tell everyone just that, so I didn't feel out of line in what I was doing. Plus, I believe that God helps those that help themselves. Dr. Tellez had told me about times that he witnessed himself accomplishing things that were outside his ability level. He felt it was through God's intervention. Just like I knew Kassie's outcome was in God's hands, I also felt that God was working through numerous people; my little voice was telling me that Kassie needed to win this fight with everyone's help, not vice versa. Dr. Tellez had told me it was up to God whether she lives or dies, that God was in control and we just had to trust Him for the outcome. I wanted there to be no misunderstandings, Kassie wants to live, and she's willing to fight for her life.

It could be that she will need this experience to prove to herself later on that she is worthy of whatever task God has in store for her in the future. Whatever God's plan might be for Kassie, it must be huge for her to be put through this large of a trial. Who knows what it could be; maybe it would involve Kassie personally, maybe it would involve another person who was saved because of what was learned by Kassie's medical ordeal, or maybe it would be one of their descendants who hadn't even been born yet. No one could know for sure, but something was at work here, there was a higher purpose. The one thing that was for certain though, Kassie would need to persevere through all of this if we were to ever have a chance of knowing what this all could mean or what it was for.

I had 100 percent confidence in Kassie's doctors, nurses, and all the ECMO techs. We had witnessed medical equipment working above and beyond their intended uses, and everything was poised toward a positive outcome. Yet there were still equipment alarms going off on a regular basis. The doctors and nurses were constantly watching for any sign, good or bad, to indicate the direction Kassie was heading. As much as everyone had done in the course of nearly a week, death was still lurking around every corner, waiting for its moment to swoop in and claim its prize.

In Kassie's life up to this point, all she needed was a goal to go for, something to set her sights on. Once she had it, she would then go about finding a way to accomplish that goal. I was always amazed that she did so with such ease. She was getting a heavy dose of work ethic now, and though some had commented their concerns with a raised eyebrow, I was fully aware that I was pushing her very hard. I had always wondered how Kassie would do if she really needed to work at something to achieve it, and I had hoped that she would really dig in and work hard. I guess we were all getting that answer right now, loud and clear. Kassie had work ethic!

*****

Coach Charlie came in to visit Kassie the following afternoon. He told her about what was going on at practice and rattled off the individual messages her teammates had given him to tell Kassie. Coach Charlie liked to stop by when he could and had already been in a couple times that week. Even though our friendship was new, I really enjoyed it when he visited. He also brought Kassie little gifts from the team, but this time he had a special gift for Kassie. Coach Charlie had gone out and purchased Kassie a ticket for the Arizona Diamondbacks Inaugural Season, Opening Day game. He explained that he was taking all the girls to the game, and even though Kassie couldn't go, she was part of his team so she got a ticket, too.

I just shook my head while I accepted Kassie's gift on her behalf. What a tremendous person Kassie had as a softball coach, what an unbelievable act of belief and kindness.

We sat down and began talking about the team, but he wanted to talk about Kassie. Was there any change? What was her current prognosis? Was there anything he could do to help? It was true that Charlie was a big man, but his heart was even larger.

"What you can do, you are already doing," I told him. "Keep the good thoughts going for Kassie, keep the team informed and involved, and please help everyone remember her in their prayers." I confided in him my fear that people would start to forget about Kassie as this draws on and stop praying for a miracle.

At that, Coach Charlie gave a chuckle and said, "Like that could ever happen! Nobody was going to forget about Kassie, she's bigger than life." I nodded, knowing exactly what he was talking about.

Charlie then told me they had won their first game the previous night, but there was a bit of a problem before the game started. Concerned, I asked what had happened.

"Well, we took the field, and our pitcher was doing her warmup pitches while the rest of the girls were throwing the ball back and forth, warming up their arms," Charlie explained. "Finally, the umpire yelled, 'Play Ball,' and the batter got in the box. All of a sudden, the umpire calls time out and tells me I'm short a player, that I don't have a third baseman, and I'd have to get a player out there or risk forfeiting the game. I told him I had a third baseman, but she's in the hospital fighting for her life right now. I've talked it over with the girls, and they all agree that third base is Kassie's position. We'll play without a third baseman for the first inning as a show of support for her! If that's not all right with you, we'll forfeit the game! The umpire looked at the opposing coach, and yelled, 'PLAY BALL!'"

Elated, shocked, excited, perplexed, and happy, I just sat there shaking my head. I couldn't help myself; tears were building up in my eyes, and I was literally choked up. "Charlie, why would you do that?" I asked. "Kassie was only practicing with you for a week when she got sick. It's not fair to your other players to risk a forfeit."

He looked at me and said, "It was the girls' decision about the third base thing. And as for me only knowing Kassie for a week… well, that's about six days longer than was necessary for me, and everyone else for that matter, to realize Kassie is a great and special person. You just tell her that we're thinking about her, and we all want her to get well real soon. And you tell her from me that I'm waiting for her to come back to the team. Her position will be right there where she left it!"

To which I replied, "The heck with that, you tell her yourself!"

While I knew that Charlie realized the chance of Kassie walking out of PCH alive was a huge long shot, and the chance of Kassie actually returning to the team was an even a greater long shot, he never let on to me or the girls on the team that was the case.

*****

More specialists were coming in to visit Kassie every day. They would confer with other doctors in the room, then smile and tell us what a miracle girl we had as they waved good-bye to leave. Nurse Arva Bynum said that someday Kassie was going to be written about in all the medical journals for what she was doing right now. Arva was Kassie's main nurse and was very easy to talk to. She had befriended our family and knew us all by name. Arva was very positive about Kassie's ability to recover and felt positive that Kassie was going to overcome all of her adversities and be okay. She would, however, always temper her comments by also saying that there was still a long road ahead for Kassie to get through. Then Arva would continue, "She's strong though, and there is definitely something different about this room. When you walk into it, you feel it, and it's definitely different. Kassie's going to pull through, I just know it." She had known our doctors for quite a while and would tell us how lucky we were to have them. That's when we found out that Dr. Tellez loved key lime pie, so of course, I called my brother immediately and had him bring in a pie for the doc, along with the daily pastries he brought to PCH on his way to work very early in the mornings every day, sometimes even before it was light out.

All the nurses who worked with Kassie were great. While they were standing on the top step of the stairs next to the bed administering care to Kassie, they would talk with us about things that were going on with them or their families. They also appreciated how we treated them, and talked with them, and told them stories of our family too. Not just stories of Kassie's adventures, but those of Autam and Stevo also. I would even throw in some old stories about when I was a kid in Oklahoma and some of the crazy stuff we had done in our lives.

One time, I told them that I was so thankful Kassie was related to our old dog Ginger.

They looked at me and said, "WHAT? Kassie is not related to a dog!"

I continued, "Just listen! When I was a little kid in Oklahoma, our family had a big boxer that we named Ginger. My dad knew a guy, and the guy told my dad that he had to get rid of his dog because it was killing the chickens of his next-door neighbor. Pop said he would take him and had great fun with the dog. He would put Ginger up in the cab of the work truck wearing a hardhat and put a pipe in the dog's mouth to finish the look. Pop was a Roustabout in an oilfield and used to kid that Ginger wasn't even the ugliest guy on the crew. One summer, the family went on vacation to Phoenix to visit with our cousins Ron, Linda, and Kenny, Uncle Aubrey, and Aunt Mary

Ann, and afterwards on the way back home detoured down to our relatives in Crowell, Texas, and they had fighting chickens. Well, my Uncle Bill told my brother Steve that if he got in the cage with the mama chicken and her chicks, and got one of the chicks away from the mama, he could keep him. So in Steve went fighting the mama hen for one of the chicks and managed to get one out of the coop. He got scratched up pretty good but had won the chicken fair and square and wanted to take him home. Pop told him that Ginger would kill the chicken and reminded Steve how it came to be that we got Ginger in the first place. Steve would have none of it and said Ginger wouldn't hurt him, 'cause it was Steve's chicken. Well, they got the chicken home, and Steve kept them separated pretty well. As winter rolled around, Pop had put a light bulb in Ginger's doghouse to help keep him warm, as snow was on the ground, and Oklahoma gets wet cold snow. One morning, Pop was leaving for work and Ginger came out of his doghouse, stretching and getting ready to hop up in the truck. That's when Pop saw the chicken come running out of the doghouse. My dad just about split a gut laughing. We got Ginger because he was killing some guy's neighbor's chickens, and there Ginger was now sharing his doghouse with Steve's chicken."

We all laughed, but the nurses were standing around looking at each other. One of them finally said, "Well, that was a really funny story, Dave, but how does that make Kassie related to a dog?"

I smiled and said, "It doesn't. I just wanted to give you a little background on Ginger before I tell you why Kassie's related to him."

They all chuckled shaking their heads, giving me the nod to go ahead and start.

I told them, "One time, Ginger was down at the bottom of the oil camp where we lived. As he started across the road, a guy came whizzing through in a little Nash Rambler at the same time. The car hit Ginger and threw him a ways up the road. While Ginger was trying to get up, the Rambler hit him again knocking Ginger forward, and then hit him again, and then again before the guy could get the car stopped. The guy got out of his car to assess the damage. He had a busted grill, a dented steel bumper, a broken radiator, and two busted headlights. When he turned to see what he had hit, he saw Ginger hobbling off the road heading home. He was pretty bunged up. The crash had knocked off all of his toenails, and he had a bad road rash, but he survived the crash—a crash that would have killed most dogs. He hobbled around for a while, but before long he was back to being himself again. The moral of the story is that Ginger survived something that would have killed any other dog, just like Kassie is going to survive something that would have killed any other kid."

The nurses asked in amazement, "Is that story true?"

"Yep, it is," I said, while raising my hand and flashing the Boy Scout hand signal. They all nodded their heads and agreed that indeed, Kassie truly must be related to that dog.

The nurses would tell us they enjoyed working with Kassie. They felt the same as Arva, that there was a different feeling in her room, and it made them feel good about being there. They commented about how unbelievable it was for Kassie to still be fighting, and that everyone was talking about the Miracle Girl on Four. They knew there was no guarantee that Kassie was going to make it, but anyone within Kassie's earshot never said anything other than that "Kassie making it" was exactly what was going to happen.

*****

Autam got to Kassie's room at the hospital after school just as the ECMO Team was finishing "Racing the Track," which was what we called it when the ECMO Team cleaned everything, while making sure nothing bad happened with the tubes connected to Kassie.

Autam began talking with Kassie about how her friends thought Team Red and White was cool, and her teachers were all pulling for Kassie to get well. She said, "I told them that if there was anyone who could survive this, it was you, because of how athletic you are and when you put your mind to doing something, it gets done." Then she began to tear up and said, "Kassie…if this had happened to me, I don't know if I could do what you're doing…but as long as you keep fighting, I'll be right here next to you helping…because that's what sisters do for each other. They help each other." Autam mustered up a smile for her little sister and continued, "I brought you some new rewards for reaching the goals I set for you last time. You have a new nail polish and a couple of candies. They are in your Elmo bag, and all of your rewards will be here for you when you wake up. Kassie, I love you, sis. Please keep fighting and coach Team Red and White to victory. I *want* you to get well and come home. I *need* you to get well and come home." With that, she pulled out her own personal transparent nail polish and began painting Kassie's toes and fingers.

I commented that Kassie would be wondering why she had clear on if she were to wake up right now, and Autam explained that she had gotten permission from the nurses to put polish on, but only if it was clear.

Autam and I laughed, and she said that Kassie would think that was boring. Then Autam let me know that the nail polishes she had given Kassie as rewards were bright colors that Kassie would definitely enjoy.

Kassie's teachers continued to come to the hospital and read to her. They would tell her about what was going on in class and who was doing what. Then they would plug in her headphones so she could hear her classmates taking turns reading to her.

Aunt Saunie began shooting a video from her camcorder because she said Kassie would never believe all the stuff that was in her room if she didn't see it for herself. She started by recording the equipment and Kassie in her bed up on the stilts, then the walls with all the great personalized memorabilia that had been sent in. She talked with the nurses and ECMO Team, then went out into the hall and the nurses' station, and down to where the entrance was to the ICU, all the while talking into the recorder to Kassie. I thought that was a great idea. The next time I went home, I grabbed a Polaroid camera and a bunch of film. Upon my return to the hospital, I began taking pictures of everyone who had anything to do with Kassie from the time she got to PCH and had them write their name on it. I also took a picture of them with Kassie for them to keep. Lorrie brought in a book that we could put all the pictures in. From that point on, if there was a new person that got involved, they got their picture taken for us and a picture together with Kassie for them. Some tried to beg off, but we wouldn't let them. If they entered the room, they got their picture taken…even the doctors.

*****

Kassie was nearing the end of her ten days of ECMO treatments, and still there was no confirmation by the doctors that they felt Kassie would survive once taken off life support. Although I was excited and happy that Kassie was nearing the ten days and was still alive, everyone was apprehensive about what to expect once she came off ECMO. Would her lungs be healed enough to absorb enough oxygen to support herself? Would her veins repair themselves where the cannulae were attached? Would she be addicted to morphine and go through withdrawal? Would she wake up and not know who we were? Would she wake up at all?

Late at night was when I would have the most time to talk with the doctors and nurses. One night, I was talking with Dr. Mike about how much rehab time he thought Kassie would need once she woke up. He had just begun stating that he wouldn't be surprised if she would still need upwards of three months intensive therapy to get her back to where she could go home, when Kassie's alarms started going off. Kassie had developed a fever, and it was getting dangerously high. Her body was beginning to show the signs of being on ECMO so long. I guess this was answering my earlier question about leaving her on ECMO longer if necessary. They began trying to cool her body down. Her temp was 107, and I was beginning to come unraveled. My stomach was getting the same feeling from before when Kassie crashed, and we almost lost her.

Dr. Mike explained that the fever showed Kassie was fighting an infection and that high temperatures actually assist in killing the germ causing the infection because it can't survive being that hot. It's just Kassie's way of showing us she's still in the fray, and her body doesn't want to be sick anymore. He said we don't have anything to worry about as long as it doesn't go any higher. She's in the best place in the world for her to be right now so we can monitor what's going on.

Dr. Mike's words made me feel a bit better, but the nurses' faces and attitudes were telling a different story. When they looked at me, they smiled, but you could tell it was a forced smile, and they wished Kassie didn't have that fever.

I went to Kassie and started telling her a story of when I was a boy. "Once when I was really little, I watched a movie called *The Birds*. By today's standards, it probably wouldn't be all that scary, but back then it was. I had only been in bed a few hours when I woke up crying from a nightmare. My daddy got up and we went into the family room where we had watched the movie. I was holding onto him so tight because I was so afraid the birds were going to get me. He told me I needed to calm down and stop crying because everyone was asleep, and they needed to get their rest so they could get up early and go to school. But I was too afraid to stop crying. I tried but I just couldn't stop. Truth be told, my daddy had to get up earlier than everyone else, but he walked around the house with me tightly clutching his neck and with my feet wrapped around him, as much as they would go anyway. He started talking to me about what he did at work the day before and about some really weird-looking bugs that he had found while he was working on one of the oil rigs. Slowly, I began to ask him some questions, and he told me all about what the bug looked like, how long it was, what color it was, and things like that. I was still very afraid, so when he tried to set me down on the chair, I held on even tighter and wouldn't let go. I knew that as long as I was in my daddy's arms, nothing could get me. So he held me tight and continued talking to me. After a while, he said he wanted to look at the TV guide that we had gotten out of the *Seminole Producer* newspaper, and he asked if I wanted to help him look at it. I said okay, and he sat down with me on his lap. As we looked at the different shows that were going to be on the following day, he asked me what shows I liked and why I liked them."

"Kassie, do you know that we sat there until we read the entire week of shows? That took a long time, but by the time we were done, I wasn't afraid anymore. My daddy asked me if I was ready to go back to bed, and I said I was. My daddy worked very hard, and he had to get up very early to go to work, but he sat there with me nearly all night so I wouldn't be afraid. Your grandpa never complained or got grouchy with me. He just did his job, happily. I want you to know that I will sit here with you as long as it takes, so you will know that you don't have to be afraid either. Daddy's here, and I'm not going anywhere. I don't have to go to work tomorrow or the next day or even the next. My boss told me to take care of my little girl, and that's what I'm doing. You just keep on coaching Team Red and White and getting them where they need to be, and Daddy will be right here when you win the race."

Truth be told, I always felt that if I could be half the dad that my dad was to me, my kids would have the best dad ever. I continued telling her stories about when I was young until the sun was nearly coming up. I told her about the time when a bunch of us were playing in the horse pasture behind our house, and a horse tried to run over me and my friends. Jerry Childers and I jerked our youngest friend over the fence just before the horse got to him, nostrils flaring and eyes as big as saucers. I told her about the time I was crawling around above the garage in the attic of an old abandoned house, when I stepped wrong and fell through the ceiling. Then I told her about the time when I first started playing football, and we were scrimmaging the older boys' team. I was playing for the youngest bracket of the Seminole Tiny Chiefs, and we were scrimmaging the next age bracket up. Their star running back went around the end and was running right towards me. Even though I really didn't know how to, I reached out to try and tackle him and accidentally grabbed the ball. I told Kassie that all of a sudden, everyone was yelling at me to run, so I did. I was holding onto the football with my right hand, holding my football pants up with my left hand, and running as fast as I could with my helmet bouncing up and down on my head. I was dodging people and jumping over piles of guys until I made it to the touchdown. I told her I must have been a sight, because along with people cheering, almost everyone was laughing or at least smiling at the spectacle they had just witnessed. Back then, you didn't have designer uniforms like you have today. You just played with what you had, and in my case, it was stuff that was way too big for me. But I didn't care, I was playing football, and I had just scored a touchdown against the older kids. I laughingly said, "I bet those guys could have played pro, after all they were ten-year-olds! Sure they were big and strong, but I guess they just couldn't handle the Arner speed."

As I was finishing my story, Kassie's fever finally broke, and her temperature started to get closer to normal. I praised her for being a great coach. We could tell Team Red and White was working tirelessly for her. I announced to those in the room that I was going to take a quick break and for everyone to carry on without me, playfully waving my hand above my head as a king might do while addressing his court. As I walked toward the door, I got a hug from each of the nurses who were there with us that night. I walked out to the corridor feeling amazingly good just as Uncle Steve was arriving with the morning pastries and muffins for everyone. He wondered what he had missed and asked if I had been telling stories again. I just gave him a wink, smiled, and kept on going. Man do I love being a dad.

*****

As the ninth day of Kassie's treatment rolled around, Dr. Liu and Dr. Tellez came in to talk with Lorrie and me. One of the concerns I'd had all along was regarding the quantity of drugs that Kassie was on in order to keep her in a coma throughout the ECMO procedure, and whether she would run the risk of being dependent to the point of going through withdrawal. We didn't want that for her, and the doctors didn't either.

They explained that once Kassie got through ECMO, they would begin weaning her off those medications a little at a time.

"What will that mean as far as Kassie waking up, how long will it take to have her come out of the coma?" Lorrie asked.

The doctors responded honestly, "We don't know exactly. Kassie has been through a very traumatic event. She has had ten days of machines doing the work for her. While the meds have kept her safe and asleep, they have likely had an effect on Kassie's body as well. Just exactly how much, we don't know yet. It could still be a couple of days after we take her off ECMO before we know more."

I gave a solemn sigh. "I guess that means you're not watching Kassie's 'Kid's Race Against Drugs' video today then, are you?" The doctors had stated they weren't going to watch the video until Kassie was out of the woods. So every day since, I asked the doctors, "Is today the day you are going to watch her video?"

To date, the answer had always been, "Not yet, it's too early to tell."

As they again shook their heads no, I asked very pointedly, "Do you think Kassie is going to wake up?"

Both of the doctors shrugged while shaking their heads, and Dr. Liu said, "I know you are both tired of hearing this, but we really just don't know."

Dr. Tellez continued, "As you know, this is the first time we have used this technology on a patient of Kassie's size, but the fact that Kassie has survived this long can only be viewed as a positive sign. How much damage the lack of oxygen Kassie sustained has yet to be determined."

Dr. Liu again spoke, "Honestly, just like you, we are all hopeful and waiting to find out if this has been worth it. Please don't misunderstand, we all think it has been worth the effort, and we all have grown to really like Kassie. What I meant to imply was whether it will yield a positive outcome."

Lorrie and I nodded that we understood his meaning, and we reaffirmed how appreciative we were for their efforts.

At about that time, Dr. Bernes came in, and we caught him up on the previous conversation. He was in agreement with the conclusions.

I asked him, "How long before you will be able to get a true reading on Kassie's brain activity?"

He responded, "Within the next day or so when ECMO is finished, I should start getting some preliminary info, but until she is completely free of the drugs, I won't have complete information to share. We know she has some brain function from when we reduced her meds before, but I'm sorry, I just can't tell you how Kassie will be until she wakes up. What damage, if any, won't be determined until then."

Day 10 arrived. It was the weekend so we knew there were probably going to be a lot of visitors for Kassie, some we would know, and some we wouldn't. The great thing was, as word continued to spread about Kassie's dilemma, there were more and more people praying for our little Longshot to receive a miracle and allow her to live. Again, I thought, *If there was a light that showed up in heaven representing the person that was being prayed for, surely Kassie's light would have to look like the sun by now.*

I prayed, "Please God, don't let us fall one prayer short of a miracle for Kassie. Please let it be your will that Kassie survive this sickness and deliver her back to us, retaining her health and mental faculties."

As I looked up from my prayer to God, I was happy to see Coach Charlie come in. He had just dropped in for a few minutes to say hi and tell Kassie to keep fighting. Then Miss Marbaugh came in with a book to read, and others arrived and visited. The crossing guard from Kassie's school came in with a beautiful handmade doll that belonged to her daughter. She explained this was her daughter's favorite doll, and she asked her mom to give it to Kassie from her. Its detail was impressive, and it was nicer than anything I had ever seen in a store you could purchase. We set it in a high place of honor and asked her to thank her daughter for caring so much about Kassie that she would part with her favorite doll. The groundskeeper for the school came in and sat with Kassie for a while. He had been at Moon Mountain Elementary School for a long time and had been groundskeeper there even when I attended the school. A couple of fellow sales agents dropped by on their way to work. A few of my friends and their families came, then the normal onslaught of all my family. More and more people came and went. The nurses would shake their heads in amazement at how many people continued to visit the Miracle Girl on Four. I was thankful that everyone we knew at PCH had also asked their family and friends to pray for Kassie. It was getting down to crunch time, and I felt blessed that everyone was continuing to keep Kassie in their thoughts and prayers.

Again, I thought, *How painful this will be to everyone involved should Kassie not survive.* I contemplated what just ran through my mind and realized how negative that was. So I shoved that out of my thoughts and replaced it with, "How wonderful it will make everyone feel to know they had a hand in helping Kassie to survive, while witnessing a miracle from God." As each of Kassie's visitors came and went, Lorrie and I personally thanked them for coming in, and further thanked them for their continued prayers and for those of their friends praying for Kassie as well. We asked them to please pass along our thanks to their friends the very next time they spoke with them.

My thirty-six-hour shift came to a close, and Lorrie was twelve hours into hers, when I finally left the hospital with Autam at 8:00 p.m. to catch some sleep at home. Autam had been there almost all day setting new goals for Kassie to attain and talking with her about what was going on in her life. As Autam and I drove home, we chatted about how glad we were that Kassie would be coming off ECMO tomorrow.

It would be a busy day again with visitors, and I asked Autam if she was going to go with me in the morning back to the hospital.

She said she would definitely be there and had already arranged to go with Grandma and Grandpa.

After eating the dinner that Caren had prepared for me, I was able to spend a few hours with Stevo, then wandered around doing a few things on numerous projects I had going on before I finally went to bed around 1:00 a.m. As I laid down on the bed trying to think of anything else I could do to help Kassie, I realized how exhausted I was and decided to put it in God's hands, so I prayed.

> Dear God, I want to thank you for my family, and please help me to continue down the

path you would like me to follow. I ask that you continue to work with the doctors and nurses at Phoenix Children's Hospital to help Kassie make a full recovery, and to remind them the work they do is important, and that many children are alive today because of their actions. Please Lord, let it be your will that Kassie survive this, and please return her to us like she was before she got sick. I also ask that you watch over my family and friends, and those who are praying for Kassie to receive a miracle from you. Please let them know in their hearts how much I appreciate their prayers to you. I also ask that you help me to think of anything that would enhance Kassie's chances for survival and a complete recovery, especially with her lungs and brain. I know this a lot that I ask, but Kassie is innocent and deserving of your presence. God, please answer my prayers. All of these things I pray in your name. Amen.

As I drifted off to sleep, I thought, *God, if I left anything out of my prayer that I should have put in, I know you already know it anyway, please forgive me. Amen.*

When I awoke the following morning, Caren was telling me that Lorrie was on the phone from the hospital.

I snapped to full awake and picked up the cordless. "Hello?" I graveled out.

Then clearing my throat, I heard Lorrie say, "Everything is okay. I just wanted to fill you in on the doctor visits that have occurred this morning."

I looked at the clock, it was already 10:00 a.m. I asked, "Who came in?"

Lorrie let me know that Dr. Gong had come in, as well as Dr. Bernes. "Both of them said that Kassie was doing very well and felt that she would be ready to come off today." She continued, "While the doctors did their rounds this morning at the shift change, there were a few more people than normal in Kassie's room conferring with Dr. Mike, Dr. Liu, and Dr. Tellez. Nothing out of the ordinary to report though…except…everyone's in their red scrubs today!" she exclaimed.

I said that was good news, and that I was going to hop in the shower, grab a bite to eat, and then head on down.

We said we loved each other, and out of bed I went thinking, *It's going to be a busy day, and I'm already late. Kassie will be wondering where I'm at.*

When I got to the hospital, Saundra was standing next to Kassie explaining all the new Beanie Babies that were there. She was telling her their names and what they looked like and what they liked to do. Aunt Saunie was great at talking to Kassie; she always had an upbeat message to relay and talked in great detail about what they were going to do together when Kassie got released from the hospital. She also rotated the Beanie Babies around, placing them in Kassie's hands, or laying them on her chest and shoulders, watching out for anything that could happen.

"Beanie Babies were very good at keeping the bad things away," she told Kassie. Saundra had just delivered a large bunch of Beanie Babies to the preemies that were on ECMO at the hospital. She said they needed the Beanie Baby magic also. Saundra had been watching out for other people for as long as I can remember. She has a kind heart and will always do whatever's necessary when a friend is in need. That's probably why I love to kiddingly needle her about how mistreated I was when she babysat me when I was a kid. That always brought a raised eyebrow and a comment, "Oh yeah, David, I remember how mistreated you were," from her.

When I was little, if Mom or Dad had something they needed to do, Saundra was usually the one that got saddled with me. Obviously, on the weekend, free babysitting wasn't high on the priority list of a good-looking, popular teenage girl. She always had plans made to hang out with her friends. Mom and Pop would say to Saunie, "Okay fine, go out with Debra, but you have to take David with you." Keep in mind, there were nine years difference in age between us, so when she was sixteen and finally getting to enjoy a bit of freedom, I was seven years old. We had moved into town from the oil camp where we lived in a shotgun house, which was a pretty basic mode of living consisting of a rectangle with a front and rear door. Now we lived in a regular house with its own yard. Saundra was a cheerleader and was very pretty and popular in high school. Seminole wasn't a very large town, so on the weekends all the kids would drag Main Street for entertainment. It went something like this...

Saundra and her best friend Debra would drive from our house and start at the new Sonic Drive-In, cross the street and go around Herman's Pig Stand, hang a right and go through Crazy Corners onto the brick street next to the Ford Garage. From there, get onto Main Street by hanging a right next to Claude Darling's store, then down the street past Newton Walls and the Seminole Producer. Make a U-turn at the train depot and head back up Main Street, driving by the movie theaters and Anthony's, then make a left when you got to the Rexall Drugstore, back through Crazy Corners by my uncle's car lot called Honest Bob's and on to the Sonic, circle it, and start all over again.

Not that I would ever get to see it though because I always had to lay on the floorboard when I was with Saundra and Debra, so nobody would know she was babysitting me. I did peek out the window sometimes by hiding behind our dog KoKo. He was a poodle and had his hair cut so he had a topknot; he kind of looked like one of the Beatles. I knew where I stood in the pecking order of things; the dog got to ride in the back seat with his head hanging out the window, while I got to lay on the floorboard. I didn't really mind though, because it was much better than sitting back home watching TV with my parents or going to bed. Plus, Saundra had hot girlfriends, and they all thought I was "the cutest." I know this for a fact, because every once in a while, I would pop up from the floorboard when Saunie stopped to talk with somebody. I would put on my best smile and proclaim, "Hi, I'm David! You sure are perty! You should come over to my house and visit, we got Cokes and everything." To which they would reply, "Well, isn't he just the cutest!" Usually, the dog would be licking my face by this time because I had ice cream or candy all over it. Saundra would give me goodies as my reward for staying on the floorboard. Pop always had eight or nine cases of Coca-Cola around. He would buy them on sale and just keep them stored, so I never worried there wouldn't be enough Cokes on hand in case someone ever took me up on my offer.

My brother Steve had a completely different approach. He was two years older than Saundra and was obviously much smarter because he would prominently display me in the back seat, and that would inevitably draw in the girls. They would want to know all about me, what my name was, what grade I was in, and how old I was. I would answer their questions and then say, "You should come over to my house and visit, we have Cokes and everything!" And my brother would smile and agree. They never did, but a lot of the time they would just get right up in the front seat with my brother, and we'd go have a Coke at the Sonic. I liked mine with cherries in it. After a while, he would ask the girls if it would be okay to drop me off at home before taking them back to their car, because it was getting pretty late. I always thought those girls were awfully nice and considerate to make sure I got home safe and sound, especially since a lot of the time their car was just parked right next to my brother's at the Sonic or across the street at the Pig Stand. I offered to have them come in for another Coke, but they always said it was too late. They told me how cute I was and that they were sure I had lots of girlfriends—of course, I didn't—but I never let on to them they were wrong. As they drove off, I thought, *I wonder if I should have told them I didn't have a girlfriend, they might come over and visit more often.*

The nurses loved hearing our family stories, or at least they acted like they did.

I thanked Steve and Saundra all the time for wearing Mom and Pop out by the time I came around. They would nod their heads and say, "Oh yeah, rub it in, you had it made!" And they were right. Steve was kind of my hero. He was the coolest when I was growing up. He played on the high school football team, the Seminole Chieftains. He had his own car, and he got to sleep in a separate room that got built onto the shotgun house we lived in at the oil camp. Before moving to town when I was seven, Steve moved to Texas to go to school, and then after that, he went into the Navy and served on an aircraft carrier. My brother was always sending me cool stuff he got at some port they were at. One time, he sent me a folding Buck knife for Christmas. I opened the box and unfolded the knife. It was almost as long as my arm. I jumped up and yelled, "COOL! I wonder if it's sharp," and promptly sliced my thumb open. At first, it didn't even hurt because the blade was so sharp, then the blood started coming, and Mom had to take me to the bathroom to fix me up. Inside the box, the card read, "Merry Christmas, little brother! Thought you might be able to use this fighting off the girls, ha. Be careful it's sharp. Love, Steve."

My brother and sister always enjoyed having our kids around, and our kids loved hanging out with them also. They liked going to Aunt Saunie's because she always had some activity going on or some goodie she had baked for them. Plus, they could play with the cats, go swimming, and play with my nephews' Nintendo and Sega games.

They liked going to Uncle Steve's because they got to do everything they weren't supposed to do. They would watch scary movies that were rated R, listen to adult alternative music with unedited lyrics, eat candy and popcorn, and drink Cokes until they were sick. When they came home, they would tell us all the fun stuff they did. Lorrie finally said it would be best if she just didn't know what they were up to when they were at Uncle Steve's.

My brother and sister were at the hospital giving support to Lorrie and me every moment possible. I couldn't even imagine my life without them. That was one thing that Mom and Pop really drove home, the importance of family. They were at the hospital every day for us unconditionally. They sat with Kassie, while Lorrie and I went to the cafeteria for a little while. It was good to occasionally get a break from the alarms that were continually sounding in Kassie's room.

As Lorrie and I sat in the cafeteria, we caught each other up on what all had occurred in the previous few days at home. Since we were never there at the same time, we would need to have a pow-wow occasionally to make sure we both knew what was happening with Stevo and Autam. Autam was pretty good about keeping us informed, but we had to pry info from Stevo. The phrase, "It's like pulling teeth to get any information," must have been invented just for Stevo. Stevo was seldom in trouble, and he got good grades, so if you weren't careful, you may never hear anything about what was going on because he certainly wasn't going to offer any information. This wasn't for any reason other than he just didn't figure it was worthy as news. In his mind, day-to-day stuff was boring, why would anyone even care? We tried to get it across to him that we wanted to know all about his day, even the boring stuff, but he would just shrug it off and say, "Yeah right, Dad."

HABITS

I was getting phone calls from workmates giving me encouragement and filling my emotional bank account over and over again. I couldn't help but think that God must have put me on the path to Shea Homes to help me and my family make it through this unbelievably trying time. I was so thankful that through Shea, I had been introduced to Stephen Covey's *7 Habits of Highly Effective People*, as I used them now on a daily basis. They are: Habit 1: Be Proactive, Habit 2: Begin with the End in Mind, Habit 3: Put First Things First, Habit 4: Think Win-Win, Habit 5: Seek First to Understand, Then to be Understood, Habit 6: Synergize, and Habit 7: Sharpen the Saw. The Habits helped me to keep my sanity and gave me a compass to follow.

These seven habits really set the tone for how I approach many aspects of life and parenting. Overall, don't be reactive in your life, be proactive to teach the correct way of doing things, then trust your kids to do them. My biggest parenting philosophy. It goes to show, even though we tend to jump into expecting the worst, exactly the opposite is most probably the case. I got quite a bit of practice using the habits with my kids, and some even rubbed off on them.

One time, while I was at work, we got a phone call from the school saying that Stevo was in the principal's office because he threw a rock that hit a kid. I just about exploded! He knew better than to do stupid stuff like that, and by the time I saw Stevo that evening, I was about to blow a gasket. However, *seeking first to understand and then be understood*, I decided to ask some probing questions before ripping him a new one.

I asked, "So, Stevo, did anything exciting happen at school today?"

"No, not really," was his response.

"Hmm, that's weird because I got a phone call from the principal's office today. Do you know what that was about?"

"Yeah, I had to apologize to some kid today."

"And why did you have to do that?" I requested.

Then Stevo explained, "Well, Dad, we were on the playground running around playing soccer, and I was standing off to one side waiting for them to pass me the ball. I looked down and saw a rock, picked it up, and threw it off the field so it wouldn't hurt anybody. We were playing kind of rough, so I didn't look before I threw the rock, and it hit some kid."

Well, this wasn't going the way I had planned at all. I had been upset most of the day because Stevo threw a rock at somebody, and he was darn sure going to remember not to ever do that again. Now I'm finding out it was an accident. He didn't throw a rock at somebody on purpose, the rock just happened to hit somebody. Now I was torqued off at myself for:

1. Believing Stevo would actually throw a rock at somebody when he knows how dangerous that could be.
2. For being mad all day over nothing, something that I knew better than to do before attaining all the info about what happened.

"So, Stevo, what did you learn by all of this?" I asked.

"To not throw rocks," he scoffed, saying so in the fashion kids do when they are repeating what they have been told a thousand times by their parents.

I had to keep myself from laughing at the way he responded. "What should you have done instead?" I asked him.

He kind of cocked his head and looked at me, not sure how to respond. "Not thrown the rock without looking first?" he responded in a questioning tone.

I said, "Well, yeah, you could have done that, but you're not really supposed to throw rocks, are you?"

"No."

"So what should you have done instead?"

He thought for a second, "I guess I should have just left it there."

I slowly said, "I suppose you could have just done nothing, but then you wouldn't have accomplished the task that you were first concerned with. Somebody might have fallen on it and gotten hurt, right?"

"Yeah."

"So what might you have done instead of throwing the rock, or just letting it sit there where somebody could get hurt from it?" I asked again.

"I guess I could have put it in my pocket, or held it in my hand until I got to the out of bounds."

"There you go! That would have been a much better choice than throwing the rock, especially without looking where you were throwing it. That was a pretty lamebrained thing to do, huh?"

He nodded yes, that it wasn't the smartest thing to do.

I gave him a hug and told him I appreciated that he didn't want somebody to get hurt, but he really needed to think things through before acting, even in the middle of a game when you are concentrating on other things.

He smirked and agreed, and I told him he could go out and play with his friends.

Today was a big day, and Lorrie and I took a moment to evaluate all that had happened in the previous days since Kassie was admitted to Phoenix Children's Hospital. The list was long, and the emotional aspect was overwhelming. Yet here we were, still on our feet, and there Kassie was, still doing her part to stay alive and continuing to fight against the Green Team. We couldn't help but wonder what the following days would bring. Would there be an outcome that could be deemed anything short of a miracle? All we could do was hope for the best…and pray.

As the doctors made their rounds at shift change, the ECMO team was preparing Kassie for Dr. Teodori to take the cannulae out of Kassie's neck and leg. It was determined that Kassie would stay on the vents to give her additional oxygen and to see how things go while she was coming off her meds. Kassie's lungs were still in bad shape, and it was inconclusive how much damage there was, or how it would affect Kassie's recuperation. Dr. Teodori was impressed with how well Kassie had tolerated the procedures and wished us good luck. I gave Dr. Teodori a long hug and thanked him for all that he had done to get Kassie to this point in time. We snapped another Polaroid for him with Kassie. We then asked if we could be in the room while he did the procedure. He looked at us, knowing he shouldn't let us stay, but he also felt that Kassie deserved to have us with her if she were to die on the operating table. Due to the blood thinners Kassie was on for ECMO, the chances of Kassie running into problems were elevated. He told us we could remain in the room, but if we fainted, nobody was going to help us. With that, we all entered the sterilized makeshift temporary operating room where Kassie had resided the last ten days.

Dr. Teodori

Dr. Gong

Although Kassie's cannulae procedure was much different than his normal actions as a heart surgeon, he completed this challenge as quickly and efficiently as he had started it ten days earlier. I assured him that his efforts would not be in vain and that Kassie was going to pull through. He smiled at both Lorrie and me, then responded that he felt she would, too. He shook our hands and headed off to a surgery that he was scheduled to perform, waving as he went, but then he paused, turned around, and came back. As he approached, Lorrie and I were looking at him in a questioning manner, wondering what he was doing. He offered his hand to both of us again and said, "You know, you really have quite a spectacular little girl in there.

I really believe she is going to come through this with flying colors. You both should be very proud of what she has accomplished." He again smiled at us, and while Lorrie and I thanked him for saying so, he shook our hands and turned to hurry off to his next surgery.

Now that Kassie was getting off ECMO, the doctors and nurses could start weaning her from the morphine and stop the blood thinners. It was unclear how long it would take for the medication to be out of her system enough for her to regain consciousness. All we could do was wait.

As the ECMO team was finishing up their process of taking down the ECMO equipment, Lorrie and I gave them each a heartfelt thank-you for being so professional and making sure everything went smooth for Kassie. We had become very good friends and felt close with each of them. We gave them huge hugs as they left, requesting that they please ask the rest of their team to come up when they had a chance so Lorrie and I could personally thank them for doing their part. We snapped Polaroids with Kassie for them to keep as a reminder of what a great job they did for the entire perilous ten days that Kassie was on ECMO and invited them to come back once Kassie wakes up so they can be properly introduced. They all said they felt like they already knew Kassie, but it would be quite an honor to actually talk with her once she wakes up.

Kassie's room was beginning to look different. Not only was the ECMO equipment gone, which was the first thing you saw in the room as you walked in, but also her bed could now be taken off the stilts, and the steps the nurses needed to administer to Kassie were taken away. The entire backside of the double room was still filled with medical equipment, but the front side looked almost normal. Gone were the dramatic effects that made up the first impression of the Miracle Girl on Four's room. Still there, was the actual girl, Kassie, in her slumber but vigorously fighting with every ounce of energy she could muster on the inside.

*****

Kassie was woefully behind in her race against the effects the bacteria left inside her body, yet she had managed to close some of the gap on her adversaries and was entering the third turn on the back stretch. Team Red and White was motoring on with Kassie as their coach, now on seemingly fresh legs, while the Green Team, big and strong, kept lumbering at their methodical pace. They snidely acknowledged to each other as they rounded the fourth turn. "We have too large of a lead for her to catch us. Our sneakiness and treachery gave us such a large head start that there's no way Kassie can possibly catch us! Nobody ever catches us." They chuckled as they were heading down the straightaway toward the finish line and ultimate victory. They barely even glanced over their shoulder to see how much ground Kassie had gained on them. Thank God they were as stupid as they were big and strong, or they may have taken additional measures and applied more treachery to secure their victory.

*****

Again, there was a constant stream of physicians and specialists filtering in and out of Kassie's room. We also still had many well-wishers coming by to see the Miracle Girl on Four, congratulating us and Kassie that she has survived the ten days of ECMO.

The anticipation for Kassie to open her eyes was just about unbearable. The doctors had said it may take a day or two, or even more for Kassie to wake up, but I wanted her to wake up right away. I wanted her to see that we were here, right where we had been from the very beginning. I wanted her to know how much we loved her and how proud we were of her for staying in the game against the most horrific odds. I wanted her to be awake and be my little "Longshot," my new nickname for her that she had never even heard. I wanted her to be happy and healthy and the same little girl she was eleven days ago. I wanted things to be normal. Still, there she lay, motionless, expressionless, and seemingly inattentive to the goings-on of her surroundings. I wanted everyone to see the little girl they had heard the stories about. I wanted them to witness Kassie in all her glory;

her pizzazz, her humor, and her mesmerizing, addictive, contagious smile.

Day 12 ended with no signs of waking up from Kassie. But on the upside, the alarms on the equipment that were still connected to Kassie were not sounding as frequently as before. Maybe Kassie would survive this, but I couldn't be sure yet; the doctors still wouldn't watch her "Kids Race Against Drugs" Tractor Race video.

Dr. Gong showed up bright and early on day 13 to see how "our" girl was doing. I told him still no change, but we were optimistic that today may be the day.

He pondered the question before asking, "How about Kassie's brain activity, has there been any encouraging news to that regard?"

"Nothing yet, unfortunately." I sighed.

He said to me, "Keep thinking positive. It has worked to this point, don't stop now."

I nodded my head in agreement, but he could tell not knowing was eating me up inside. I really needed Kassie to wake up and show me she was okay. I couldn't eat or sleep; afraid I would miss being there when she first opened her eyes. I worried she would wake up, not knowing where she was, and she would be scared. I didn't want her to be scared. I wanted and needed to be the first face she saw. There would be a lot of time for the faces of others. She would need to know she wasn't alone among strangers, even though at this point they were anything but strangers, but Kassie wouldn't know that. More of her daily X-rays were being done, and we were seeing there was improvement with her lungs. How much of the damage would be irreversible was yet to be determined.

A little later, Dr. Bernes came in to see how things were going. It was obvious he had taken a shine to our little Kassie. He asked, "Still hasn't woken up yet huh?"

I shook my head. "No."

"It may be another day or more before that happens. Remember, she's been through a very traumatic experience."

Of course I knew that, but it was somehow reassuring to hear from a knowledgeable person that it was okay she hadn't woken up yet. Lorrie and I remained vigilant the entire thirteenth day, hoping and praying today would be the day. Alas, again, the day wore on, and it was not meant to be. Each second seemed like minutes, and each minute seemed like hours. It was exhausting. Lorrie and Autam finally headed home. I spent the rest of the evening speaking with the caring doctors and nurses who continuously streamed in and out of Kassie's little corner of the world in Phoenix Children's Hospital.

They felt, as I did, Kassie's room was removed from the rest of the world, and the goings-on of everyday life were inconsequential while in her room. It was its own little universe. Nobody had time for tiny unimportant things like world peace or the like; there was one task and one task only on everyone's mind, Kassie's survival and full recovery. It was on everyone's face, and it felt good they were on Kassie's team.

I slept restlessly the entire night, partially due to anxiety, partially due to exhaustion. At times, I would toss and turn, not being able to sleep; at other times, I would wake myself up from snoring so loud. I was embarrassed that while everyone around me was working so diligently in the care of Kassie, they had to deal with my snoring. I had heard that it was impossible to snore if you were lying on your stomach. Well, I definitely busted that myth. The nurses laughingly told me not to worry about it, as they continued on their seemingly never-ending journey of excellence.

Day 14 started, and amazing as it sounds, I actually felt kind of rested. My eyes were stinging like I hadn't slept, but I had optimism in my heart that Kassie was going to wake up today. The morning turned to afternoon, and I was fiddling around rearranging Kassie's get-well cards, stuffed animals, and letters, so anybody who wanted to could see them more clearly. It seemed we were constantly rearranging the stuff on Kassie's walls to find more room to add more stuff as it arrived. As I did this, I was talking to Kassie, telling her what I was doing, reading excerpts from the cards and letters, explaining which stuffed animal I was moving where, and why I was doing it. I was telling her that I was working as fast as I could to make things look great because I knew that she was going to be waking up soon.

I reminded her to continue coaching Team Red and White, and that it was more important than ever to keep fighting.

*****

Kassie was putting every effort into catching the Green Team. She had rounded the last turn and was in a full sprint for the last 70 or 80 meters. The spectators in the stands couldn't imagine where Kassie could possibly be drawing her energy. Were they witnessing an upset in the making? The Green Team was over halfway down the final straightaway with only about 40 meters to go. They were already celebrating and taunting the crowd by screaming, "WAAAA!" and rubbing their cheeks as if they were wiping tears away. They were giving each other high fives while yelling out smack and making obscene gestures toward the crowd. All the while to the Team Green's delight, the entire crowd was booing and hissing them. Maybe that's where Kassie was drawing her energy, everybody cheering for her and booing the Green Team. Kassie's eyes were as big as silver dollars as she sprinted down the straightaway toward the finish line, but there was no smile, her face showed only a look of determination. She remembered her daddy's words, "There will come a time when you will have to do more than just show up to win." She gritted her teeth through the pain and moved herself to lane four, her favorite lane, and sped stealthily toward the pack. The Green Team was grouped and on its way to the finish line, but she could see they were taunting the crowd and being disrespectful. That got Kassie's blood boiling. That determined look became even more intense, and her eyes became small slits. She thought to herself as she fought through the pain, dug in and increased her pace, "These guys need to be taught a lesson, and I'm just the one to do it!"

*****

I had just finished remodeling Kassie's room and was feeling pretty pleased with the outcome. I was standing next to her bed telling her the room was ready for her to see and just then Kassie opened her eyes and tried to focus on the first thing she saw—the snarling nearly life-sized Taz balloon hovering above her at the foot of the bed. Kassie loved Taz because that's how she personified herself to be in sports. She was always tenacious with reckless abandon, in a semi-controlled fashion, ready to go from 0 to 100 miles per hour in a heartbeat.

As her eyes focused, and in the fogginess of her long slumber and medication, the outline of what must have seemed like a monster crept into her brain. Her body lurched, I suspected in fright.

As I got to her, I said, "It's okay, Kassie, it's Taz. It's Taz, honey, it's okay!"

She hazily looked at me and back at Taz, as what I said seemed to creep into her still sleepy mind. She finally focused on Taz, and she seemed to breathe an acknowledging sigh of relief; it seemed to me she then kinda shrugged and moved her head at the same time. I felt maybe as if to say, *Duh, how'd I miss that.* But was I just being hopeful? Was there any realization of what was going on? Did Kassie really understand what was going on around her, or was it just involuntary muscle movement?

I held her hand and squeezed it, catching her attention. I said, "Kassie, it's Daddy, do you understand what I'm saying?"

She looked at me somewhat quizzically and blinked her eyes a number of times, trying to focus in on me and what I was saying.

I prayed to myself, "Please, God, help Kassie to understand me and let her be okay."

I said again, this time a bit louder, probably due to apprehension, adrenaline, and excitement, "Kassie! Sweetheart! It's Daddy! Do you understand what I'm saying?"

As her eyes focused in on my face, and she looked at me, there was no expression, only a blankness.

My heart was breaking as I repeated, "Kassie! Baby, it's Daddy. Can you hear me, sweetheart?"

She shifted her head to look at me, as she did, our eyes met again. I was smiling, and she was surveying me very closely. When she looked into my eyes and nodded yes, I could see she was in there. My Kassie was still in there and she had brain function, and as she nodded her head yes again, I briefly started jumping up and down before I contained myself, realizing I was still holding her hand. I quickly touched her small face with my hand and smiled while slowly telling her that I loved her, and that she shouldn't try to talk because there was a tube in her throat. I explained that she was in the hospital, and that everything was all right and that she hadn't done anything wrong. I tried to tell her everything that would relieve any questions in her mind so she wouldn't be afraid, and that I was here with her. Daddy was here.

By that time, there were a number of nurses and techs gathering around Kassie's bed. The doctors were checking her out, taking readings, and asking her questions. Kassie seemed to be having trouble understanding what people were saying, and she sometimes didn't know how to respond. I was hoping it was due to the medication fogging her responses. It was all very overwhelming for her, and I could see she was scared, and tears were starting to come. I tried to reassure her that everything was okay, and these people were here to help her get better. Kassie's facial expressions spoke volumes. She didn't like being here, she didn't want to be here any longer, why wasn't I protecting her, and why wasn't I doing anything about all these people bothering her. She looked at me pleadingly, expecting for me to rescue her from this onslaught of doctors and nurses. Kassie had been thrust into an unknown and frightening situation, and although I was exhilarated from Kassie waking up, my heart broke from the look on Kassie's face. Suddenly, I remembered that it was because of my inaction at the very beginning that placed Kassie in this situation. Once she found out, how would I ever gain her trust again? Would she ever be able to love me in the same way she used to?

I made call after call telling people that Kassie had woken up, and that her faculties seemed to be pretty well intact. Some people wept on the phone because of the miracle that had just been witnessed, while others ecstatically chatted about how wonderful it was, and that I was right when I said Kassie was a fighter. Still, others praised God for providing a miracle and thanked me for allowing them to be a part of the tapestry that had been woven in front of us. My parent's neighbor and friend, Ruby Miller, was one of the very happiest to hear the news. She had adopted my kids as her surrogate grandkids because she and her husband, Junior, had grandkids who lived out of state. She always had some freshly baked something or other for the kids, and they loved to play at Ruby's house with her handmade dolls, or to help make saltwater taffy. Ruby had even begun teaching them how to quilt, along with many other activities she was very good at. As I told her the fantastic news about Kassie, she quietly thought to herself that she was going to have to really get busy and step up the tempo with the surprise quilt she was making for Kassie as a present for getting better. Ruby had secretly been working on it since Kassie went into the hospital.

In making the calls, my exuberance returned as I rejoiced in Kassie's awakening. People were dropping what they were doing and heading to the hospital. When Lorrie and Autam arrived shortly after the "great news" phone call, all we could do was smile, kiss, and hold hands, while Kassie, visibly unhappy with her predicament, was tended to by the nurses. We knew we had to temper our exuberance because she still wasn't out of the woods. Her lungs were in terrible shape, and her body was dilapidated. Worst of all and most telling, the doctors still had not watched her tractor video.

*****

During the fourteen days that Kassie was there, she had lost 25 percent of her body weight. She literally looked like one of the kids who Sally Struthers showed in her UNICEF commercials. Kassie had no body fat to begin with, so her body fed on muscle mass while she was in her coma. Kassie could no longer do anything for herself. She couldn't even sit up in bed, her arms would flail when she tried to move them, and she had no body control. All of this took Kassie totally by surprise. She had no idea why she was in the hospital. She had no memory of ever going to the hospital. To her, it was as if she kissed her mom good-bye for work, laid back down because she still wasn't quite well yet, and then she woke up in the hospital unable to talk, walk, or even sit up.

Try as we might since her waking up, nobody had seen the contagious, beautiful smile we had painted in everyone's mind. As a matter of fact, nobody had seen anything from Kassie except for an extreme case of her being really mad and a sense of bewilderment. When the nurses came in to take care of her, Kassie fought with them and didn't want to do what they asked of her. It seemed they were always pounding on her back to dislodge the residual effects of the gunk that was left in her lungs. They were drawing blood, giving her breathing treatments, taking X-rays, moving her, waking her up, and doing one test and then another. Although Kassie had awakened from her induced coma, everyone was still feverishly working to make sure Kassie survived her illness. Now that Kassie's lungs were on the mend, it was decided they would take away our good friends L and R, the two vents that worked together flawlessly so Kassie's lungs could inflate, and replace them with one vent they called "the Cadillac" for a couple of days, just to make sure Kassie got enough oxygen. This new vent would now be able to do the job L and R had been doing. I felt a bit apprehensive about L and R leaving after doing such a great job for us, but I was also excited they felt the new Cadillac vent could work for her and her damaged lungs.

While all of these distractions were occurring, Kassie was still running the biggest race of her life coaching Team Red and White on the inside. Throughout the night and into the next morning, Kassie was pushing herself to the limit. She was exhausted and still she battled on.

*****

All along the race track, you could hear the boo and hiss of the crowd as the Green Team would pass, and from the crowd as Kassie went by, there were huge screams of encouragement and cheers of excitement. As Kassie continued to close the gap between her and the horrible disrespectful pack of cheaters, she smartly quieted the cheers for her from the crowd by placing her finger against her lips. She needed the crowd's help. She needed the element of surprise, and the crowd responded by booing and hissing even louder to the great delight of the Green Team. The Green Team was nearing the finish line when Kassie made her move from directly behind them, and she kicked it into overdrive scooting to the outside. She remembered the Hershey track meet, and this time the outcome would be different. Her arrival took the Green Team totally by surprise. As a matter of fact, they hadn't even realized that Kassie had snuck in behind them until she pulled alongside. They were astonished when they finally noticed she was next to them. She shouted to them that if they were going against her, they would have to do more than just show up to win. Then she gave them the infamous Kassie scowl and stiff armed the leader in the face causing him to fall, and in so doing, took out the entire Green Team as they tripped over their leader. As Kassie crossed the finish line, she singsongingly exclaimed, "Cheaters never prosper!"

The crowd was going crazy as they had just witnessed the biggest come from behind victory, perhaps, of all time. The Green Team ran to the officials of the race and shouted that Kassie had cheated and that nobody ever beats the Green Team. The officials looked them up and down, then proclaimed, "No Blood, No Foul," and ruled Kassie the winner. The Green Team wailed and screamed that it wasn't fair; to which Kassie replied, "Haven't you heard? Life's Not Fair! Get used to it!"

THE INFAMOUS KASSIE SCOWL

On the morning of day 15, both Dr. Liu and Dr. Tellez came in to check Kassie's most recent X-rays with Lorrie and me. They agreed that there had been significant improvement since she first got here, and it looked as though with proper physical and occupational therapy, they felt confident Kassie was going to recover. She had truly defied the odds. Then Dr. Liu asked if they could watch the "Kids Race Against Drugs" video everyone had been talking about and further pondered why they hadn't been allowed to see it yet. The two doctors then looked at each other and busted out laughing.

Lorrie and I almost passed out; they had finally asked to watch the video. We happily gave it to them and hugged them both, thanking them for all their hard work and dedication.

I tentatively asked Dr. Liu, "I guess that means that you feel confident that Kassie is out of the woods, and she is going to survive?"

While he was nodding his head, he also let us know that Kassie would have a tough road of therapy ahead of her, but then smiled and assured us that he believed Kassie would survive.

My brain registered that Dr. Liu had given us a positive prognosis, and I was ecstatic. I assured them that Kassie was a fighter, and she would be more than happy to do whatever was necessary to get the heck outta here.

Dr. Liu commented, "If I only had a nickel for every time I have heard that Kassie is a fighter!" We all laughed as they both nodded their heads in agreement. Kassie truly was quite a miraculous girl.

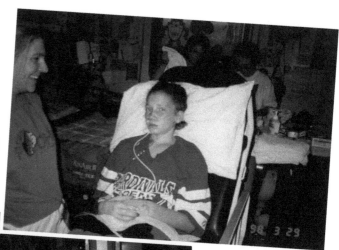

The Kassie Scowl

Aunt Saunie,
Grandma Arner,
Nurse—getting
ready for a walk

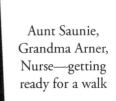

Cadillac chair—first
days out of coma

"How much time do you think Kassie has in front of her at the hospital?" I asked.

Dr. Tellez responded, "It will be hard to say, but there will be someone in later to talk with us about the rehab that will be necessary. As for now, there would be a number of days just getting her more stabilized on the fourth floor before anything else could happen."

I began to think, *Oh, man! Kassie isn't going to be here on the fourth floor much longer.* While that prospect made me happy that she would be well enough to move from there, I also felt anxiety from having to leave and go to another floor and into the regular part of the hospital, where we would have to get to know other doctors and nurses. I didn't want Kassie to leave the unbelievable care that was given on the fourth floor, and I didn't want Kassie to leave *her* nurses and doctors either. We had a comfort level with these people, and we trusted them. I was going to have to get my brain to wrap around that; thankfully, it wouldn't be happening overnight. I finally decided to deal with that as it came closer to happening. Right now, we had a job to do. Kassie was still in need of an explanation as to why she was here, and she needed all of our help to get her body back to normal.

The regimen was excruciating for Kassie. While it was true Kassie had defeated the Green Team, their effects on Kassie's body were severe. Aside from their obvious onslaught that was easily recognizable in Kassie's outward appearance, they had also ravaged her body from the inside. Her lungs were left with permanent damage and large chunks of gunk that Kassie had to expel by coughing. This would have been hard enough by itself, but Kassie still had the vent tube down her throat. When she began coughing, they would use a suction device to pull the mucus and tissue from the tube. Kassie hated that! It hurt her, she didn't like it, and she wasn't shy about letting everyone know it. Her actions were literally bringing her caregivers to tears. There is usually somewhat of an intentional disconnect between the patient and the therapists, but those walls had come down long ago. They hated putting Kassie in pain considering everything she had already been through. Kassie would look at me, wanting me to do something, and all I could do was try to comfort her by telling her she was getting better and she needed to hang in there. That day was excruciating to all of us because of the constant pain Kassie was being put through. I could only hope they would take the vent away soon. That night, Kassie got very little sleep, and she was exhausted from all the rigors she had been put through. I decided to speak with the doctors and see what they thought about removing the Cadillac ventilator.

Kassie had been on the vents now for over two weeks, and every day she stayed on them would open up opportunities for additional complications. The doctors were hopeful that Kassie's lungs had healed enough to do the job, but her left lung was still in very bad shape. Would her right lung be able to pick up the slack while the other lung continued to heal? The doctors finally decided it was worth the risk. They would take Kassie off the vent the next day and put a chest tube into her worse lung to help keep it inflated. Adding the chest tube would require some surgery, and there would be some discomfort. One thing was for sure though, it would certainly be a lot more comfortable wearing the nose oxygen than having the vent tubes going down her throat. The oxygen would now fit nicely next to the nose feeding tube Kassie had been on for two weeks; hopefully, that would be going soon as well.

Kassie was still being as somber as ever when Dr. Gong came in to see her. He explained now that the vents were removed, they would step up the efforts to clear Kassie's lungs from the residual effects of the pneumonia. He explained to Kassie that the junk in her lungs was keeping her from getting well as quickly as she would if it were not there, and that they needed to help her get it out. They would roll her onto her side and lightly pound on her back to help dislodge all the junk in there. While that sounded fairly benign, the reality was Kassie had lost a lot of weight, and she was skin and bones. So to her, that light pounding felt like haymakers, and the coughing it produced hurt her tremendously. She quickly learned to hate the percussion tapping and fought the therapist doing it. I literally had to hold her arms above the elbow to keep her rolled over. Now that the vent was removed, Kassie could kind of hoarsely speak.

The next day when the therapist arrived, she was trying very hard to yell at the therapist to stop before she had even begun, and Kassie was being very hateful. I asked the therapist to wait outside for a few minutes and for her to please shut the door behind her. Debbie, the therapist, looked at me quizzically for a moment; I nodded to her and gestured toward the door. She slowly did as I asked, while Kassie and I watched her exit the room.

Kassie looked back at me with appreciation in her expression, but she quickly noticed that my demeanor was anything but what she was expecting. I peered into her eyes and in a very low and stern voice explained to her, "All of these people, every one of them, had a hand in saving your life. They all worked tirelessly, working overtime and extra shifts to ensure that you got better. They came in on their days off to see you while you were asleep, read to you, cared for you like you were their own child. Now they are doing their jobs to make sure you get well and out of the hospital as quickly as possible, and all you do is fight them. Do you want to go home?" I firmly asked.

Kassie looked back at me with tears streaming down her cheeks and nodded that yes, she did want to go home.

I said, "I want you to come home, too, so does Mommy and Autam and Stevo and everyone else. But now you have to do your job just like everyone else has done theirs to this point. You have to do what they say, when they tell you to do it. And even if you don't like it, you have to do it as if it were your favorite thing to do in life. You have to *choose* to do everything possible to get well. These people will help you to reach your goal, how quickly you get there is up to you. Do you understand?"

With a pouty frown, she slowly nodded her head with tears now flowing like a stream.

Kassie knew by the tone of my voice this was not open for debate or conversation. I looked at her and held her small face in my hands and said, "I love you, sweetheart, and I want you to come home as quickly as possible, are you going to do as I ask?"

Kassie slowly nodded her head yes with fear of the unknown in her eyes.

I wiped away her tears and went to open the door to let Debbie back into the room. I also asked if Arva could come in and be with Kassie while Debbie did her job. I stood at the foot of the bed while Kassie hacked and coughed, she nearly threw up a couple of times from coughing so hard. After the session, Kassie was exhausted. Debbie and Arva gave her big hugs and told her how great she had done. Kassie looked at me, and I silently acknowledged she truly had done a spectacular job. I told Kassie to close her eyes and get some rest.

As I walked outside the room, Arva was there waiting. She took both my hands and gave them a squeeze; no words were spoken. I half-heartedly smiled and gave her hands a squeeze back. I then walked to the unoccupied family meeting room, went inside and wept uncontrollably, not only for what I had done and said, but also for what I had witnessed. Kassie fighting through the pain of the pounding and the coughing, no longer complaining, just doing it like her life depended on it. How I longed for the days when all it took was to kiss the boo-boo to make it all better. Then to go to whatever the offending party was, whether it was a table corner she had just bonked her head on, or the corner in the hallway she just ran her knee into, and smack it, saying, "Bad table!" or "Bad wall!" "Don't you ever hurt Kassie again, or I'll smack you around something terrible." And then smacking it again for good measure so it would know I was serious. Oh, how I hated being so helpless to defend my daughter from the pain and anguish she was experiencing. I knew I had to suck it up for her sake, and that I needed to do what I had done, but inside I was broken into a million pieces. It wasn't her fault she was in the predicament she was in, but she was feeling the full brunt of it, shouldering all the repercussions, mustering all the strength to obtain the new goal—getting well and going home. Oh, how I hate "Life's Not Fair!"

As I walked back into Kassie's room, it occurred to me that Kassie's room was getting larger. In reality, while I was out, they had finally removed L and R, the two ventilators that were so instrumental in saving Kassie's life. I knew they were inanimate objects, but I was disappointed that I had not thanked them for doing their jobs together so flawlessly before they got separated and put into someone else's room. I wanted them to know they had made a difference, even if they weren't sentient. Kassie was still sleeping from her ordeal, and I sat down next to her bed and nodded off also, thinking about how proud I was of her, and internally wondering if I would have the strength and courage myself to do what she has done.

*****

From that day forward, Kassie was the model patient, doing everything asked of her and more. How remarkable she was! How unbelievably remarkable.

Kassie awoke and I began chatting with her. Kassie seemed somewhat removed, so I asked her if everything was okay. She kind of shrugged and I asked, "What is it, honey?"

She quietly asked, "Daddy, what happened to me? Why did this happen to me?"

"Well, honey, you caught a really bad bug, and it made you very sick. You didn't do anything wrong, and you didn't do anything to get in trouble about. You are in the hospital because the bug you caught was very dangerous, but you defeated the bug with the help of everyone here at Phoenix Children's Hospital. Now you have to continue working hard to get back to yourself again."

She then asked, "Daddy, will I ever be able to walk again?"

I was dumbstruck at the question. "There is no reason to believe that you won't be able to make a full recovery from what the doctors are saying," I reassured her.

With tears forming in her eyes, she stated, "Daddy, I can't even get out of the bed by myself, or stand without someone holding me up. I can't take a step or hold a cup. I can't do anything but lay here and cough."

I held her hand, and after a short moment, I said, "Sweetheart, you have lost a lot of weight, and your body needed to feed itself fighting this illness you had. Because you were in such good shape, there was no fat for your body to use, so it had to use your muscle.

135

As you get stronger and are able to do more exercise, your muscles will begin to remember what they are supposed to do. This doesn't happen overnight. This is something that is going to take a while, and you will have to set small goals for yourself. Don't expect to be able to just make it happen immediately, don't get discouraged. This is going to take some time and a lot of effort. But you will win, you will be able to come back from this and be yourself."

"Really, Daddy?" she asked with the look in her eyes that said she really wanted to know the truth, no candy coating; she needed to start making assessments for herself and she needed the real truth.

"Yeah, baby, really," I sincerely responded.

She then asked, "Will you help me, Daddy? Help me every day?"

I smiled and said, "Of course, I will, sweetheart. I will be here, and a number of other people will be here, too, to make sure you are going to be okay."

She again looked very solemn and looked down.

"Kassie," I said and waited for a response. Kassie looked kind of like she was in a far-off place, so I repeated, "Kassie"—I touched her arm, and she looked at me—"didn't you hear me?"

She shook her head no.

"Kassie, we know how difficult this is for you. But it sure would be nice to see you smile. Everyone has been waiting to see it. Any chance you could smile for Daddy right now?"

With that, Kassie again looked down and began crying, shaking her head and saying she can't.

I said that was okay, and we'll just keep on looking forward to it. I then asked, "What is it, honey, what else is bothering you? I can tell there is something else."

"There are so many things going on, and they are doing so many things already..." her voice trailing off to nothingness.

"But?" I asked.

She looked at me very sadly, and with a tiny frown and a quivering lip, she stated, "Daddy, I can't hear very well. It's really muffled, and it sounds like everyone is very far away."

I had noticed at times that Kassie didn't seem to be paying attention, but I had marked it up to being tired, or maybe she was concentrating on something else so she didn't notice that someone was talking to her. I told her I didn't know what might have caused that, but maybe it was just a temporary thing brought on by the medication she was on, or maybe it was because she was asleep for so long that she might have some build up in her ears. I told her I was glad she told me and that I would follow up with the doctors to see what they had to say.

Shortly after that, Debbie came in to pound on her. When Kassie saw her, she gave a little wave and rolled over on her side so she could get started. What a trooper my Kassie was.

Lorrie arrived and I filled her in on what had been happening, including the hearing issue. The doctors checked her ears visually and didn't see anything obstructing them, so it was determined Kassie would be seen by Dr. Mike Sabo the following day or so to have a hearing test done. For now, there was plenty of work to do in getting Kassie's strength and stamina built up. The physical and occupational therapy was difficult, causing her muscles to ache and cramp regularly, but Kassie bit her lip through the pain and persevered onwards toward her goal of going home as quickly as possible.

Since Kassie had woken up and the vents had been removed, we wanted to find out when the feeding tube could be taken out and Kassie could get back onto regular food. The doctors were cautious not to throw too many things at Kassie since she had only come off ECMO less than a week ago, and they didn't want to introduce food until they were certain her digestive track was working properly. Kassie was still unable to get out of bed unless someone could help her. She was very weak, and her muscles were not responding very well. There was some improvement however, albeit small. They would get her out of bed and sit her in the "Cadillac chair." This was the chair they used that had restraints to keep kids from falling out of it. They strapped her in and pushed her around the pod on the fourth floor, allowing Kassie to venture out of her room for the first time in weeks. People clapped and cheered for Kassie as she was wheeled around the floor. Kassie didn't like having to be pushed around, and she especially didn't like people seeing her the way she looked.

*****

Dottie Hagan, Shea Homes

Now that Kassie was out of the woods, I went back to work. Dottie had carried me for some time professionally. It was probably too soon, but I felt like I needed to get back. The struggle that Kassie was constantly battling filled me with emotion. I hated the fact that Kassie had been thrust into this situation through no fault of her own. I hated how hard it was for her now, and more so knowing that it was going to be even harder on her while recovering. I found that every song on the radio reminded me of something regarding Kassie, and I cried all the way to work, and all the way home after work, every day. Leaving the radio off didn't work either, because my thoughts would always be drawn to what was going on with Kassie, and that it was my fault that she was in this situation. Mentally, I was a wreck. I couldn't keep my mind on things at work and was constantly being interrupted with news of some sort or another or someone was calling to check on Kassie's status. I had a large backlog of buyers, and they would come in to see how I was doing and to ask about Kassie. I could barely get through a conversation without my eyes getting misty. Thank God, Dottie was around to bail me out and divert conversations. It wasn't that I didn't want to work; I would sincerely try, but there was something missing, something I wasn't even aware of. I had lost that little spark that sets the top producing sales people apart from the rest, and it showed on my next secret shopping report when I scored in the seventies. I don't believe I had ever scored below ninety in the seventeen years I had been in new home sales.

As my boss and I sat down to watch my video shopping tape, it was like watching someone else. I missed opportunities to ask questions and determine additional info needed to help someone to make a decision to purchase. Questions I had been asking as second nature for over a decade were now just in some void. In the video of my performance where I should have been asking questions, disturbingly there was only silence, over and over again. I clearly was not performing as usual.

After watching the tape, my boss asked me what I thought.

I said that I couldn't believe that was me on the video.

He nodded in agreement and said that even though I was outwardly showing no signs of the dilemma we had gone through with Kassie, I still had a long way to go to get back to where I was previously.

One of the great things about working for a quality home builder is they provide these tools so you can assess yourself on how to be better. I definitely had a lot to work on, that was for sure. I felt like a rookie. As I drove home from our meeting, I thought how insignificant my job had become while Kassie was still going through all of this. How was I going to recapture my edge, the thing that set me apart, and how long would it take me to get it back? I hoped for all of our sakes that it wouldn't be long; but in reality, it would take me a year before I no longer cried in my car every day, and two years beyond that before my secret shop scores improved back up to the nineties again. I just couldn't get completely into work mode. I was distracted by ongoing events and humbled by the sheer magnitude of what our lives had morphed into due to the challenges that Kassie constantly had to overcome.

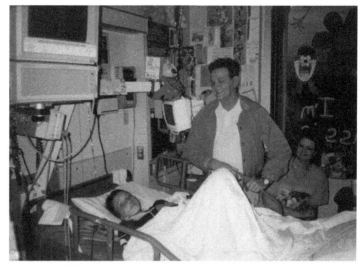

Grandpa Arner and Aunt Saunie visiting

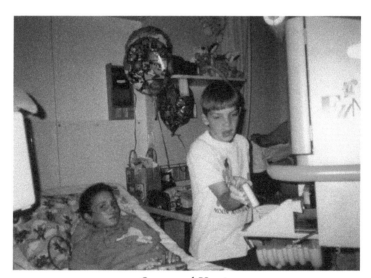

Stevo and Kassie

Later that afternoon at the hospital, Lorrie was reading *Island of the Blue Dolphins* to Kassie. Lorrie got up to do something, and when she did, Kassie's feeding tube got caught and was pulled loose. Lorrie didn't even know it happened, and Kassie obviously didn't say anything because she had been wanting it out since she woke up and realized what it was. Lorrie finally noticed the feeding tube was missing because the sheets were wet. She asked Kassie what had happened, and Kassie coyly gestured she didn't know. Lorrie called in the nurses, and the doctors discussed whether to replace it or not. It was determined that they would leave it out and allow Kassie to start eating some regular food. The doctors and nurses joked with Kassie, hoping for a smile, that they knew she wanted the feeding tube removed but taking things into her own hands was a bit forward. But still no smile surfaced, only the same noncommittal facial expression she had worn since waking up. How I longed for that beautiful contagious smile that warmed everyone's heart and set Kassie apart from others. How I wished I could see that beautiful smile again.

The following day, Autam and Lorrie were visiting with Kassie, who was sitting up in the bed being hand-fed like a little bird by her big sister. Autam was holding Kassie's popsicle for her while having a conversation with their mom. The thing was though that Autam has a little bit of Italian in her, as when she speaks, her hands tend to move. Kassie was following Autam's hand around with her mouth trying to get a bite of the popsicle; she looked like a drunk sailor with her head bobbing all over the place. When she finally got a chance, Kassie nipped at it, but she missed and got Autam's finger instead. Autam turned to her and said, "HEY!" Kassie looked at Autam and kind of half-smiled at her, which of course led to much celebration!

After that, Kassie was staring at Autam's french fries. Autam noticed and said, "Kassie, I will give you a french fry if you smile."

Kassie looked at Autam and gave another half-hearted smile.

Autam then said, "Oh no, if I'm going to give up a whole french fry, you have to give me a big smile."

To which Kassie responded by breaking into one of her huge Kassie smiles, and the room lit up, illuminated as if there were two suns battling for supremacy; the normal one outside her hospital room that provides warmth and gives life to the earth, and now one inside her room that gloriously showered anyone in its presence with happiness.

Autam gleefully asked if she would like catsup on it, and Kassie happily nodded yes, temporarily forgetting she didn't like catsup but quickly remembering once it was in her mouth. When no one was looking, Kassie removed the fry from her mouth and hid it in her Elmo bag, where all of her treasures and treats had been stored from the small goals that had been set by her big sister and then ultimately realized by Kassie. When Autam looked back, she laughed at how quick Kassie had eaten her fry and gave her another, this time without catsup though.

When I got there later, I found the gnawed upon french fry and asked, "What was up wit dat?"

Lorrie and Autam looked at each other and then at Kassie. Kassie exclaimed with a big smile on her face that she didn't like catsup on her fries.

We all laughed. It was the first time we had all laughed in so long, and it reminded me of how things should be, and how things were going to be again.

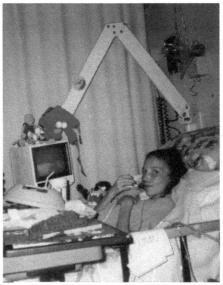

Kassie, Autam, Mom, and
Caren-Grama Nelson

Kassie eating ice cream

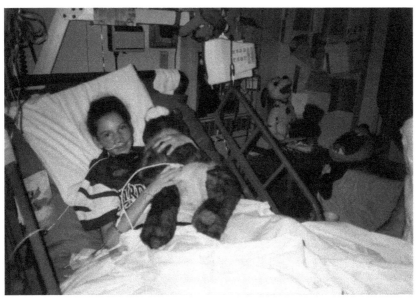

Kassie with Soft Bunny from Lisa and Bette from Shea Homes

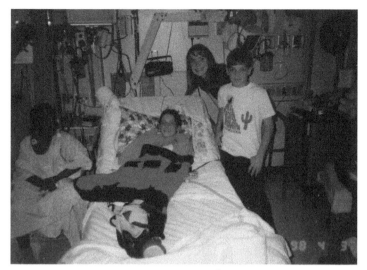

Kassie, Autam, and Stevo

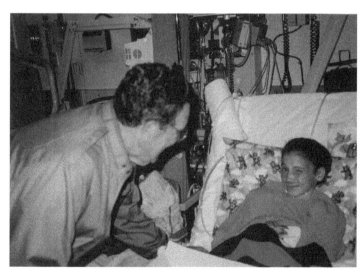

Great Uncle Aubrey teaching Kassie to wink

The real food Kassie was now eating was making a difference on her outward appearance, and within a week, she no longer looked like a walking skeleton. The food was also making a difference in her strength, and soon she was able to sit on the side of the bed and get dressed with assistance. When she stood, she could balance a little bit on her own, but her steps weren't really anything more than just dragging her feet forward a little bit while being held up, so her feet just barely touched the ground.

She was getting stronger little by little, and her personality began coming back. With a little bit of convincing on my part to the nurses, she no longer had to take rides in the hated Cadillac chair and could now ride in a regular wheelchair, as long as we guaranteed not to go around corners too quick, or stop with a jerk. Kassie said that left me out from being able to go along, which caused the nurses to laugh. Lorrie also finally uncovered the mirror that had previously been draped with a Cookie Monster poster. We had a fear that if Kassie saw how she looked, she wouldn't be able to recognize herself and that may scare her too much.

Years later, when Kassie saw a picture of herself laying in the bed on stilts, she asked, "Mommy, who is this little girl?"

When Lorrie told her it was her, she didn't believe it.

Kassie said, "Yeah right, Mom, that doesn't even look anything like me, who is it really?"

When she saw that her mom was serious, Kassie stared at the photo of this little girl lying in bed with "her" mommy stroking the little girl's hair. Kassie thought, *Surely, Mom is kidding me, that couldn't be me…could it?* She knew for sure the mommy in the picture was her mommy. Again, she scrutinized the picture and asked very questioningly, "Really, Mom? That's me?"

Lorrie attempted to compose herself, acknowledging Kassie's question with a knowing smile and a nod, all the while trying to ignore the tears and all those memories flooding back to her consciousness.

Getting onto regular food was to be the beginning of the end for Kassie's stay on the fourth floor, and soon she would be off to the next phase of her rehabilitation. Her time remaining on four would be filled with painful occurrences. From the percussion treatments thumping methodically on her back causing her to cough and gag, to the constant muscle ache that would not cease from her efforts trying to regain muscle control. Kassie was now eating anything she wanted, with our assistance, and smiles were a lot more frequent, but never a day went by that Kassie didn't tell us she wanted to go home. We knew we were a long way from that happening, and I told her from the very beginning that how long she was going to be in the hospital would depend a lot on how hard she worked on her rehab therapy. In all honesty, she worked vigorously on the things they wanted her to do and well beyond their expectations. Kassie was constantly in pain, but she didn't complain, and she never felt sorry for herself. She had a goal, and that was to get the heck out of the hospital and back home.

*****

Kassie was sent over to Dr. Sabo for a hearing test. We sat in the room with the doctor, while Kassie sat in a soundproof room with a window in it so we could see her. The doctor was to push a button, causing a sound to be transmitted to Kassie's earphones; then once she heard the sound, Kassie was to press the handheld button. My heart broke as Kassie sat there silently waiting for the first sound as the doctor pressed buttons for the higher pitches. When he got to the base tones, Kassie could hear those, but she was nearly completely deaf to the higher pitches. The next test was for Dr. Sabo to say a word, and Kassie was to repeat the same word she heard through her headphones. Kassie only repeated three of the ten words correctly. She was close on some of them but not correct. While it was determined there had been significant loss, all were hopeful that some, if not all, of Kassie's hearing would return. Per the testing, Kassie had lost about 65 percent hearing in one ear and about 55 percent in the other. More tests were done, and the results would be forthcoming.

A week went by and Kassie was scheduled for another hearing test with Dr. Sabo. Although she really liked Dr. Sabo, she very much disliked getting tested because she knew she wasn't going to do well; and therefore, she didn't want to go in the soundproof room. After some coaxing and some major tears being shed throughout the testing, her hearing had not improved. The test results had also come back and showed that the little hairs inside Kassie's ears that carry sound were no longer alive. My heart sank as the realization set in that Kassie's hearing loss was going to be permanent. Dr. Sabo saw my reaction and was moved that the news affected me so. He quickly stated there was much research going on, and there had been some successes in rejuvenating the hairs in lab animal tests. He felt confident there would be a major breakthrough within our lifetime. We also talked about cochlear implants, but all agreed that probably wouldn't be the best course of action for Kassie.

After a while, Kassie kind of shrugged it off and said she had already gotten pretty good at reading lips, which was true. She had nearly a 100 percent on repeating the words back to Dr. Sabo if she was allowed to look at him when he spoke the words to her.

I tried to shake it off also, reinforcing outwardly to myself that of the five senses, hearing was the one I would go without if I had to choose. But inside, I was reeling with the news. "How could this be? It just isn't fair for Kassie to lose her hearing after everything she has already been through."

Dr. Sabo said that Kassie would be able to hear men pretty well, but kids' and women's voices would be tough for her to pick up.

Later, after I had gotten my brain around the fact that Kassie would have permanent hearing loss in regard to women and children, I realized I had that same affliction. Mine was just self-imposed while I was enthralled in watching something on TV. I called it selective hearing; Lorrie called it rude. No matter what you called it, Kassie would have to deal with it on a much larger scale. How would she be able to interact in her classes? Would her teachers work with her? On one hand, I was so elated Kassie had miraculously survived her illness; on the other hand, I was inexhaustibly angry that Kassie was being put through such trials in the aftermath.

Caren-Grama Nelson and Uncle Steve B-day and 4th Floor departure party

Ruby hand sewing Kassie's quilt

Finished Quilt

Grandpa's picture of his Sweety Pie, signed quilt

The next day, we went to see Dr. Gong, Kassie's pulmonologist at PCH. This was the first opportunity Dr. Gong had to give an extensive examination of Kassie's lungs. While Kassie was getting set up for the examination, Dr. Gong reiterated what a miracle it was for Kassie to have survived. He also mentioned that he remembered our conversation about Kassie's athleticism and whether or not her illness would affect her abilities. He told me that this testing would help shed some light on that and at least give us a glimpse of what challenges could lay ahead for us. Dr. Gong had Kassie do a number of tests, but the one I was most interested in told us how much lung capacity Kassie had retained through the illness. After the testing, Dr. Gong informed us that Kassie had lost approximately 25–30 percent of her lung capacity, and compared to a normal child her age, she was at about 70–75 percent for the amount of air she could "push" out of her lungs.

While this news wasn't good, it wasn't terrible either. I knew that Kassie could live a normal life and would be able to be competitive...in time. I realized that the chances of Kassie ever being a world-class marathon runner were probably out of the question, but that was acceptable because I knew Kassie didn't have a great desire to be a distance runner anyway. I wasn't going to worry about Kassie running marathons when the current state of affairs was that Kassie still couldn't walk on her own and was being wheeled around in a wheelchair.

Overall, Dr. Gong seemed fairly pleased with the results considering the circumstances. He told Kassie to continue using the plastic toy he had given her that would help her lungs to get well faster. The idea was to suck air through it, keeping the little plastic balls in a certain place, while raising the doomaflotchie thingamabob to the top.

Kassie liked Dr. Gong and smiled in agreement that she would continue playing with it often.

Dr. Gong gave her a hug good-bye as we made her next appointment to check her progress in thirty days.

I knew the reason Kassie so readily agreed to use her new toy was because she couldn't stand that Autam and Grandpa could do it better than she could. I chalked it up to a healthy competitive spirit and called it good.

A few days later came the word that Kassie was being transferred from Phoenix Children's Hospital on the fourth floor to the regular hospital on the eighth floor. It was a bittersweet occasion that called for a going-away party. We brought food and desserts for family, friends, PCH staff, and everyone on four to enjoy. There were smiles, laughter, and tears. Then there were more tears and smiles when Ruby gave Kassie her beautiful new quilt made with her favorite colors of forest green and pink designs, which had already been signed by Kassie's friends, family, doctors, nurses, and staff at PCH. And then there were even more smiles, laughter, tears, big hugs, and huge waves good-bye as Kassie was wheeled away to the elevator for the last time. There truly was something very special about the Miracle Girl on Four. It was perceptible by the doctors and nurses working with Kassie from that first day, when there was only a 5 percent chance of Kassie surviving the night. It was there during ECMO and while Kassie lay motionless in a coma. It was there when Kassie finally woke up. And it was there in everyone's hearts as Kassie tearfully waved good-bye to all who had helped her to live. Kassie continued waving until after the doors of the elevator closed, making sure everyone knew she was going to miss them. Kassie cried some tears of joy, knowing she had just completed her first step to recovery by leaving the fourth floor, but mostly she cried tears of sadness knowing she was leaving the people she had grown to love. She knew they had loved her too, had cared for her tirelessly, and had helped save her life from the Green Team. It was that thought that again brought out her beautiful contagious smile.

EIGHT

When the doors to eight opened, Kassie had a new goal—walking without assistance and dressing herself. She could now hold things in her hands without dropping them, but she still could do no more than sit up in bed without becoming exhausted. Kassie also still had the chest tube in for the one lung that was the worst, and the doctors were discussing when they were going to remove it. Kassie didn't like having to wear the oxygen clip and practiced with the plastic toy Dr. Gong had given her to build up her lungs. Kassie thought she was doing it as well as could be done until Autam and Grandpa showed they could still do it better. That really lit a fire under her, and she practiced on it more than ever. Lorrie and I were told that when the chest tube was removed, it would be painful for Kassie. Since they were not sure when the removal was going to occur, we requested that they not remove it unless we were both there.

Life on eight was a lot more relaxed, the nurses were nice, and they tried to make Kassie comfortable when they could, but it was a far cry from the attention we got on four. We knew that it was going to be that way, but it was still hard to get used to the difference. There was one advantage though; Stevo could come and go with the rest of us. He would sometimes lie on the bed next to Kassie and play video games with her, before being shooed out of the bed and onto the nearby chair by the nurses. He missed his big sister; it had been over a month since he had enjoyed any quality time with her.

Since there were only two years difference between Stevo and Kassie, they hung out a lot together once Autam had started going to school. Lorrie would take Kassie and Stevo shopping with her to the grocery store or to the mall. Anywhere she went, they went, too. As Stevo began jibber jabbering, Kassie would translate for her little brother, letting Mommy know what he was saying and what he wanted. Lorrie would listen intently to what Stevo was trying to communicate to her, and finally she would just look at Kassie and ask, "What is he saying?" Strangely, Kassie always knew what it was that Stevo wanted, or what he wanted to do.

Kassie was always pretty intuitive. Even before Stevo was born, she told everyone she was going to have a little brother, which was interesting, because we decided we weren't going to find out if we were to have a boy or a girl. When asked what if she had a little sister instead, she would look all confused and say that she was having a baby brother, not a baby sister. We were worried that she would be disappointed if we had another little girl, but as it turned out, she was right all along anyway.

A couple of days after Kassie's transfer to eight, it was determined by all concerned that Lorrie and I needed to go out on a date. We hadn't had any alone time since Kassie got sick, so we decided to go out to dinner, while Grandma and Grandpa Arner stayed at the hospital with Kassie. We verified the doctor was not in and the chest tube wouldn't be removed that night, then off to our night on the town we went. We promised we wouldn't talk about anything that had to do with the hospital. We could only talk about fun things, and that's what we did. It was very enjoyable going out with Lorrie and just chatting about stuff. For the first time in what seemed like months, it almost felt like our lives were somewhat back to normal, even if it was only for a few hours. We were both acting like we were in high school, which conjured up thoughts of her tight blue PE shorts…

*****

The year Lorrie and I first met, we were seniors at Thunderbird High School in Phoenix, and we both worked full-time jobs. We had early bird PE and both the girls' and boys' classes were doing something outside on the volleyball courts. While I was waiting in line for a pen to use so I could write something down regarding whatever it was we had just completed, a buddy of mine pointed this chick out to me and made a comment as to how fine she was. I agreed and noticed this chick was also using a red pen. Well, red was my favorite color, so I went over and took it from her.

Quite surprised, she looked at me and asked what I thought I was doing.

Since taking her pen was as far as I had gotten in my planning process, I began to freewheel an explanation. I believe I mentioned before that I am a "No Guts, No Glory" kinda guy; so I responded by saying, "I needed it to write something down."

"Couldn't you have waited until I was done using it?" she asked.

To which I responded, "No, I needed it for something very important, and it couldn't wait."

"Oh really!" she mused. "What could possibly be so important that you couldn't have waited until I was finished using it?"

"I needed it to write down your phone number," I said and gave her my best innocent smile, looking right into her eyes.

At which point, she of course rolled her beautiful eyes at me while looking at her friends in a scoffing way, then glanced back to see if I was serious or just goofing on her. I was a bit of a jester, and I guess I did have a bit of a reputation. But there I stood, with pen at the ready in my hand. She looked directly back into my eyes trying to scrutinize the situation. Thank goodness it was October, and there was a chill in the air, or I might have busted out in a sweat. After an eternity, and others still waiting to use the pen, she grabbed the pen from me, then grabbed my hand and wrote her number down.

Of course, I was now "The Man," and my friends were shaking their heads and patting me on the back. All I could think was, "Man, am I glad that actually worked!"

I had just pulled off the biggest heist of my life getting Lorrie's phone number.

Meanwhile, I was also working forty-plus hours a week in the evenings and seldom got home before midnight, sometimes because of work, sometimes because of sticking around after work to help close up with my friends, and maybe partying a little bit. So I guess it shouldn't have come as a surprise to me while walking down the breezeway at school one day a couple of weeks later, when all of a sudden, there was this girl in my face asking me if my finger was broken. After taking a step back and realizing it was Lorrie, I honestly told her that I worked a lot and that I just hadn't gotten around to it. She was mad, and I could tell that I had made a serious error in judgment by not calling sooner. I quickly apologized but explained if she wanted to see me, she should come to where I work. Again, she looked me right in the eyes and scrutinized what I was saying. I didn't wait and told her where I worked and asked her to come and see me. I was a shift leader and would like to introduce her to my friends. I gave her a little more info and that seemed to suffice, so off to class I went, wondering if she would really drive across town to see me and hoping she would. I couldn't wait to show her off to my friends! I had told them all about her. They were beginning to wonder if she was a figment of my imagination. Thank goodness, my buddy Mike Hadley worked there, too, and backed my story up.

Working in a pizza parlor had its advantages. You will never go hungry, and there is never a deficit of interesting people to either watch or make fun of. For a guy who had just turned seventeen, it was always a target rich environment for the pretty girls, too. Being as cool as we were at seventeen, my friends and I determined we needed to devise a covert way of letting each other know when there was a pretty girl to check out. It had become obvious when you would say something to get the guy's attention and five guys would come running out from the back kitchen to stare at the poor girl. During the dinner rushes, it was quite common for all of us to lend a hand at the different workstations if one of us was caught at the register or on the phones. Job number one at a pizza parlor, don't burn the pizzas. We had four gas-burning "Blodget" ovens, and we used them all during busy times. It became commonplace to hear someone say to check one or two or three or four, depending on which oven the pizzas were in. I decided that check five was our code word, and that anyone witnessing a pretty girl had the obligation to allow all of us to enjoy the view by saying, "Check five please." If you were interested in taking a peek at the pretty girl, you would casually walk to an oven, open the door, then in as uninterested a fashion as possible, check her out. This worked out perfectly, and all was good in the universe once again.

We were all working a busy Friday night when one of them called out, "Check five please!" As we all turned to look, there stood Lorrie thanking him for the complement. I had previously warned Lorrie about our code word and had let her know she would probably be ogled a bit when she got there by our merry band of jocks and jokesters. I introduced Lorrie to everyone, and she fit right in with my handpicked group of high school degenerates, so I guess it was inevitable that we would be together forever.

*****

It was fun holding Lorrie's hand during dinner and while we were walking around.

Someone even asked us if we had just gotten married. They were shocked when we smiled and said, "No, we have been married seventeen years." Then I laughingly followed it up with, "It probably seems a lot longer to her though."

That brought a smack to my arm from Lorrie, exclaiming, "It does not!" and the people laughed.

When we got back to the hospital, we found out the chest tube had been removed, and they botched it twice before finally getting it out. Kassie literally looked like she had been put through a ringer, and so did my parents. Although they tried to hide their frayed nerves from us, we could tell they weren't happy about what had happened. It immediately became apparent there was a huge difference from being on the fourth floor to being on the eighth floor.

Did these new people not realize what Kassie had been through? Did they not realize what our family had gone through? Did they not hear us say, "Do not take the chest tube out without both of us being here?"

The blissful evening we had just enjoyed was gone in an instant, and I was seeing red. I felt like making a huge scene for all to hear and see, but instead I went to the people at the desk and asked to speak to whoever had removed Kassie's chest tube. I was informed they had already left, and I spoke to the assistant instead.

He explained the chest tube had gotten stuck, and the skin had attached itself to the tube, so they had a hard time with it.

I asked if anyone had told them we had requested to be there for the procedure since we knew it was going to be traumatic for Kassie.

"No, we were not told that," he said. "We asked if the parents were around and were told they were out. Normally, it's just a quick procedure so we decided to go ahead with it. We didn't realize how long the tube had been in place until we got started."

As I calmly listened to him, and with my entire body about to explode, I decided the best course of action at this point would be to just walk away and see Kassie. I then began my quest to get Kassie moved. The eighth floor wasn't working well for me.

SUBACUTE

Thankfully, we were on eight a very short period of time, just two days, when it was decided that Kassie would be moved to the "Sub Acute" unit, which was the area where kids who were healthy enough got moved to continue their rehabilitation. There they would lay the groundwork to ultimately allow Kassie to go home.

Kassie was returning to her old self more and more every day; the same little Kassie we loved so dearly. However, with that came the fact she wanted to go home more and more every day. I met with the rehabilitation specialists to give them a little insight on what made Kassie tick. I told them if they wanted to maximize her efforts to get well, all they needed to do was tell her that nobody had done this particular task in such and such time, or covered this much ground in such and such amount of steps.

"She needs to have a goal to work towards," I said. "That is how she is wired, that's how she sets her goals, to be the best at something. It doesn't even matter what it is. She just wants to do it the best."

They thanked me for the input and said they had a program set up for her to follow.

Indeed, they did have a complete program all laid out for Kassie. They worked on her arms, on her balance; they worked on her strength and stamina; having her practice standing from a sitting position in a chair; and they increased each of the tasks as she continued to build up her strength. Soon, she was trying to take steps on her own, but her muscles had atrophied so much that she wasn't able to lift her feet. To give her some extra practice, I would also work with her in the hallway outside her room in the evenings after I got off work. I would stand facing her while holding onto her hands to help her balance; all the while praising her for her efforts and loudly whispering encouragement to her as she teetered with her balance. At the beginning, we would just stand there for a bit, and she would get so exhausted from trying to keep her balance that she would have to sit down in the wheelchair I had brought out into the hall with us. The muscles in her legs just couldn't remember how to walk. I told her it was okay, and it would just take a little more time and practice. I assured her that I was here for her, and we would work on it together. Truth be told, I relished the time Kassie and I spent together. It gave me a sense of purpose, and I was dedicated to the idea that Kassie was going to recover completely from this.

She nodded up at me from the chair and rested for a couple more minutes, then held out her hand for me to help her stand. She took a couple deep breaths and closed her eyes, focusing on the task at hand. When she opened her eyes, there was that familiar determined look I had seen hundreds of times before—that look she got when she was getting ready to really put her mind 100 percent into whatever it was she was about to do.

In that very millisecond, it hit me. Kassie was attempting to do something that I just took for granted. Something you don't even have to think about, something that was as easy to do as shaking a friend's hand. Kassie was literally having to teach herself how to walk again. I really hadn't fathomed the magnitude of her situation. I just figured she would get stronger and start walking. I didn't realize that she had physically lost her ability to walk. This changed things in my mind. I wasn't there to steady her while she took her first steps, I was there to coach her how to walk again; my strategy would need to change.

As Kassie took another deep breath getting ready to start, I looked into her dark brown eyes filled with determination and said, "Kassie, listen to me. I want you to focus on your right foot. I want you to lift your foot a little and just move it forward a little bit, and set it down again."

She nodded her acceptance without changing expression and, while holding my hands, lifted her right foot and set it down again.

We both looked at her foot and saw that it hadn't moved forward.

As she sat back down in the wheelchair, she shook her head and exclaimed, "I thought I had taken a step, Daddy. Why didn't it work? I told my foot to take a step."

"I'm no doctor, sweetheart, but I don't think your foot was listening." As Kassie smirked at my remark, I continued, "Maybe it's gotten so used to not having to work that it has forgotten how to listen. Maybe you should tell it out loud to step forward." That suggestion brought a little giggle from Kassie, and I smiled as big of a smile as I could muster.

After a moment, Kassie was ready to try again. She stood with a bit of help from me, took a couple of deep breaths, closed her eyes, reopened them, stared into my eyes, and very determinedly, albeit somewhat quietly said, "Left foot, step!"

Neither of us looked down but continued to stare intently at one another. I finally raised my eyebrows, glanced both ways as if I were checking to see if anyone was looking, and peeked down at her feet. I looked back up and kind of smirked like I was ashamed I had looked down and gritted my teeth, while looking off to the right through my squinted eyes.

Kassie finally said, "Daaaddy! Well?" as if waiting for me to say something.

I looked back at her and, in a glancing motion, flipped my eyes downward and back up to her eyes, then downward and up again, raising my eyebrows and motioning with my head for her to look down. We both slowly dipped our heads downward toward Kassie's feet. Her left foot had moved ever so slightly, but it had definitely moved about the length of her toes forward.

With that, she looked up at me and stated tearfully, "It looks like we have our work cut out for us on this walking thing."

I nodded and agreed, and then I suggested we try it again, this time with *me* telling her foot to move. I explained that because she still wasn't very strong yet, her voice was still sort of quiet, and maybe her left foot just hadn't heard her well enough to take a good step.

Kassie intently nodded her head, and we looked into each other's eyes again. We took a deep breath together, and Kassie closed her eyes.

I waited for her to reopen her eyes before I said very sternly and quite loudly, "Kassie's right foot…step forward!"

As Kassie and I stared at each other waiting for the magic to happen, Kassie's attention was averted behind me. Apparently, my command drew the attention of the nurses down the hall, and they were standing in the middle of the hallway looking at us. Kassie cracked a smile and sheepishly looked back into my eyes, her face full of apprehension and suspense. She almost couldn't contain herself as she began bouncing her head a little bit, trying not to bust out laughing.

I questioningly opened my eyes wide and glanced down as if asking whether she wanted to look down.

In response, she opened her eyes very wide and smirked back as if to say, *Yes already! Let's look!*

Again, both of our heads slowly dipped forward to view her right foot's toes slightly ahead of her left foot.

If Kassie could have, she would have hopped up and down, and I would have loved for her to do so, but instead I was perfectly content to see that huge contagious smile that was beaming from Kassie's small face.

I picked her up and whirled her around and sat her back in the wheelchair exclaiming in short breaths like I had just run a 400-meter race. "I've had enough exercise for today! I need to rest."

Kassie looked into my eyes, pursed her lips together, and shook her head knowing that I was just saying that so she would rest and not overdo it after such a huge undertaking.

I knew she wanted to try to do more, but I wanted to make sure we ended things on a high note, and I could tell that she was worn out, even if *she* wouldn't admit it.

I turned to the nurses in the hall and waved at them. They smiled, shaking their heads, and waved back. With that, I spun Kassie around 180 degrees in the wheelchair and popped a wheelie the length of the hallway back to her room, which drew shrieks and squeals from Kassie all the way into her room. I supposed my antics were a bit juvenile to others, but I didn't care. I had a new job number one, and we had begun our trek to walking unassisted. From that day forward in subacute, Kassie did her therapy with the specialists, and then she and I had our own little therapy session together, unbeknownst to anyone else.

*****

Kassie was doing well in therapy, and her specialists were happy with her progress.

I would sit there and watch what they had her doing, all the while thinking to myself, *Tell her nobody had ever balanced sitting on the big blue ball for sixty seconds before losing their balance.*

But instead, they would tell her good job, that time you balanced for twenty-three seconds.

I quietly sat there and kept my mouth shut, while internally I was plotting out what Kassie and I were going to work on next.

Within just a couple of days, she had gotten stronger. Kassie was now able to take two half-steps in a row, then three, then four. While it was true that Kassie was only able to move her foot about four inches per step, she was gaining confidence with her stamina. Kassie never missed an opportunity to tell the doctors and nurses she felt like she was ready to go home. She became so insistent that finally her doctor told her that he would come by in the next day or so and go over some parameters on what needed to occur before she could be released to go home. Kassie saw this as a small victory and was pleased with herself that soon she would be going home. Now she would know what was required of her, and she could set her mind to accomplishing any of the challenges that were set before her. I was worried that once she found out what was required, she might become disheartened because of the possible difficulty.

I received a phone call that afternoon from some very good friends, Will and Donna Wilt. Their son, Cody, was on Kassie and

Stevo's football team that I coached. They had finally gotten word about what had happened to Kassie and wanted to know if it was okay to come for a visit, or maybe even come by after dinnertime. I told them that would be fine, and we would love to see them but wanted to make sure they knew that Kassie was going to look a lot different than what they remembered. Donna confided in me they had heard the message on the answering machine and had gotten the gist of what was going on. I briefly filled her in on what had happened, and the magnitude was overwhelming to her. She was even more determined to come and see Kassie after our conversation. I thought it might be kind of fun to see if we could borrow one of the meeting rooms to have dinner together and told Donna I would call her back shortly. I called Lorrie, and she agreed it would be nice to do that but had reservations about how Kassie's appearance might affect Kassie and Stevo's friend. We talked it through and decided that Cody was mature enough to not stare and make Kassie uncomfortable. I contacted the nurses' station and asked permission to have dinner in one of the meeting rooms for our family and some friends. They absolutely loved the idea and said it would be great to do that. I was somewhat surprised at their quick answer, and I asked them if they had to check with a doctor first or anything.

The nurse in charge smiled and said, "Sub Acute is run a little bit differently than a hospital. The reason Kassie is at Sub Acute is because she is well enough to start getting better with some added touches."

"Like therapy?" I responded.

Then she finished by nodding and adding, "And having occasional dinners with friends and family. That will be a great morale booster, and the happier Kassie is, the quicker she will get better."

I nodded in agreement and thanked them for understanding. I called our friends back and made dinner plans for the next day.

The following morning, Kassie was on pins and needles, waiting for the doctor to come and see her. Her room was the last one at the end of the north hallway. The nurses' station was about a hundred feet away, and the hallway extended south the same distance past the nurses' station. There were about twenty rooms in the entire length of the hallway, and the doctor always started at the other end and worked his way toward Kassie's room. Kassie had told the nurses that she was finding out today when she could get out of the hospital because the doctor was bringing her a list of what needed to be done. Kassie sat in her wheelchair and peeked around the corner all morning, catching glimpses of the doctor as he worked his way toward her. Lorrie and I were anxious to find out what the terms were as well, and we were hopeful that Kassie could come home for Easter. We knew though that getting out of the Sub Acute after only three weeks must surely be an impossibility. Early on, we were told that Kassie would probably need two to three months' worth of physical therapy before she would be able to go home. Still, we could only hope for the best.

Finally, after what seemed like an eternity, especially for Kassie, the doctor came into her room. He chipperly asked, "And how are we feeling today?"

"I feel good enough to go home!" Kassie responded.

The doctor smiled, shook his head looking at us, and exclaimed, "Well, she certainly is consistent."

Lorrie and I knowingly nodded our heads in agreement with a half-smile on our faces.

The doctor looked at Kassie, then said as he looked downward toward his notebook, "The nurses said you wanted to talk to me about something?" His face was noncommittal as he scribbled something else in his book.

Kassie looked at him, then back to us, then back to the doctor again before exclaiming, "Yeah…you know…the list you were making for me so I would know when I was getting out!"

The doctor looked up at Kassie, and with a surprised look on his face, said, "Did I say I was going to give that to you today?"

Kassie was so shocked by his statement that she was literally speechless. All she could do was sit in her wheelchair with a bewildered look on her face and her hands thrown into the air while shooting glances back and forth between us and the doctor.

Then the doctor got a big smile on his face and said, "Oh! Do you mean this list?" as he pulled the piece of paper from his pocket.

Kassie let out a big sigh like the weight of the world had just been lifted from her shoulders, and a smile crept onto her face knowing she had just been punked hook, line, and sinker.

You could tell the doctor really liked Kassie and respected her for her work ethic and determination to go home.

He then said, "I'm going to give you this list to keep, but I'm going to go over it with you first, okay?"

Kassie said, "OKAY!" and the doctor began reading the list.

1. You have to be able to dress yourself without any help.
2. You have to be able to go to the bathroom without anyone helping you.
3. You have to get released from your physical and occupational therapy specialists.
4. You have to start going to the hospital school and have the teacher agree it's okay for you to resume studies on your own.
5. You have to continue to eat enough food to make you strong enough to resume normal activities at home.
6. And lastly, you have to walk the length of the hallway to the nurses' station in less than a hundred steps…without assistance and without stopping.

With that, the doctor wheeled Kassie to the hallway and had her stand up. He said, "Let's see how you're doing with your walking."

Holding one of the doctor's hands, she faced him and began taking some half-steps forward while he stepped back a little at a time. I followed with the wheelchair and after about ten steps, Kassie had gone about five feet and needed to sit down to rest. The doctor was impressed she did as well as she had, and he told her so.

Kassie looked up at him and shook her head. "I'll get better at it," she proclaimed somewhat out of breath.

Sub Acute recovery—door to room

Kassie gaining strength in the hallway

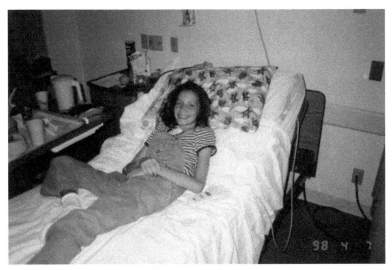

Kassie chillaxin' in Sub Acute

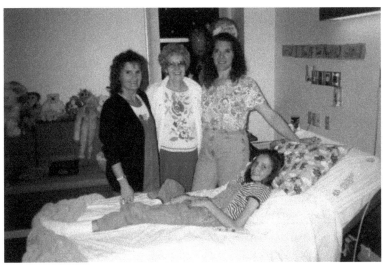

Kassie, Caren-Grama Nelson, Grandma Arner, and Mom

As Lorrie wheeled Kassie back to her room, I thanked the doc for giving her some goals to work on.

He smiled as he shook my hand and said, "Absolutely remarkable!" as he turned to head down the hallway.

I suddenly decided to seize the opportunity and walked after him. "Hey, Doc," I called out. As he turned back around, I asked, "How would you feel about allowing Kassie a day pass so she can come home for Easter? We could have her back in eight hours." The doctor looked at me like a deer in the headlights. I could tell that question hit him totally unprepared so I added, "Or whatever time-frame you would allow."

He stammered as he said, "We don't normally allow that, but I will discuss it and get back with you."

I told him I would appreciate anything he could do to make it happen, and that I felt it would do Kassie wonders to get out, even if it was for a short period of time.

He said he would check into it and waved good-bye as he headed down the hall.

As I turned to go up the hall in the opposite direction, I reminded myself, "The answer's always *no* if you don't *ask*." I decided not to tell Kassie of my conversation with the doctor; there was no use getting her hopes up for something that probably wouldn't happen.

That evening, we had a special treat by having friends in for dinner. Kassie was excited to have some new company, and Lorrie and I were happy to have some outside conversation that wasn't completely overshadowed by Kassie's circumstances. Cody, Kassie, and Stevo chatted about all sorts of stuff having to do with mutual friends and the upcoming football season. It was at that time that I realized I had missed the Coaches' Interview over a month ago. I was embarrassed that I hadn't even thought about it until then. I was later told of how upset the board was that I hadn't showed up for the interview, and the fact that I didn't even call to let them know I couldn't make it made things even worse. Luckily, word had gotten to them a short time later, probably by our friend and neighbor, Julie Tewers, about what had happened and all was forgiven. As a matter of fact, the Pop

Warner North Association even sent over a huge bouquet of flowers for Kassie expressing their concern and their hopes for a speedy recovery. I was happy they understood my uncharacteristic behavior and wanted me back to coach, even without the interview. I was also happy that football season was still months away. Maybe we could get into a routine of normalcy by then. The Wilts and the Arners enjoyed a meal together, and the kids had a good time. It helped us to further realize that Kassie was still a very social person, and outside interaction was a tool we could use to help Kassie get better.

Even though Kassie had her wheelchair with her, she wanted to walk back to her room. She made it some of the way before Cody talked her into sitting in the wheelchair so he could push her the rest of the way. Never once did he make fun of how she looked or how different she was from before. She still acted goofy and fun, so he took it all in stride and helped make Kassie feel normal. As they left, the Wilts expressed to us that they would be more than willing to help out getting the kids back and forth to activities, and made us promise to keep them in the loop as to how Kassie was progressing. I was very glad they had called and was even happier that we had dinner together. I was also very impressed with Cody's maturity toward the situation and was proud to be coaching such a fine young athlete.

Kassie continued giving her all during physical and occupational therapy, working on the other items on her list from the doctor, and also covertly doing our secret father/daughter therapy sessions late in the evening when there was limited staff. Lorrie was worried I was working her too hard, but I assured her I was being careful and watching her very closely to make sure she didn't overexert herself. I knew there was a fine line between working someone to push themselves and pushing them past the point of exhaustion.

Head Coach Dave, Cheerleader Kassie, Football
Player Stevo, Pop Warner Shredders

Kassie wanted to go to the hospital school with the rest of the kids that were in Sub Acute, but it seemed her therapy sessions always ran into that time frame, and she needed to rest after therapy. This concerned Kassie greatly because without the teacher's okay, Kassie couldn't get released from the hospital. Finally, at the end of the week, Kassie made it to class and made the best impression on her teacher she could. She apologized for not coming to more classes and asked if maybe she could make up any work she had missed, or maybe the teacher wouldn't mind coming to her room occasionally to verify she was doing her work. The teacher confided in me later that the school was there more for interaction than it was for teaching, and she could tell Kassie would be fine missing classes to attend therapy sessions. The teacher was very good at teaching multiple grade levels, and Kassie enjoyed interacting with the other kids. Some of those kids were terminal patients, and it amazed me that their spirits were always so high. They loved life, and they persevered through their hardships for the small amounts of time when they felt good enough to interact with the other kids. Kassie was eager to strike up friendships with her new comrades and easily slid into the daily grind of school. Her days were certainly full, and she needed to take breaks to rest and sleep, but each new day brought new energy and determination.

*****

As Good Friday rolled around, Kassie was sitting in her wheelchair peeking around the corner for signs of the doctor to make his rounds. She liked it when the doctor came in because she always got a good report card from the therapists, and she really enjoyed how the doctor made such a big deal of how well she was doing. I had left a message to talk with him before the weekend regarding the requested day pass, which of course was still unbeknownst to Kassie. Kassie wheeled around in her chair and announced that the doctor was at the nurses' station. She had a big grin on her face and was giddy with anticipation, then went back to peeking around the doorway. The doctor was almost to her door when she peeked around the corner. She sucked in a deep breath of surprise and hurriedly backed up out of the doorway toward the bed. I thought it was funny that Kassie didn't want him to know that she looked forward to his visits and that she impatiently waited for him to arrive.

As he sped in through the doorway, he sternly said, "I hear someone in this room doesn't think it's fair that I start at the other end of the hall and work my way down to this end of the building. Is there any truth to that?" Kassie had casually mentioned to the nurses a few days before that she hated that she was in the last room, and that the other kids were lucky to be down at the other end of the hall.

Kassie was totally taken by surprise, and all she could do was say, "Daaaaddy, I told you not to complain so much!" As she glanced away from the doctor, she pleadingly shot me a look to cover her back.

I playfully stammered, "I…er, ah, ummmm… I just wanted to make sure I got to see you before I had to go to work."

Kassie tilted her head and smiled as she looked back toward the doctor, happy she had been exonerated from the accusation.

The doctor looked away from Kassie toward me, winked, and said, "So it wasn't some other person in this room that wants to see me before anyone else does, huh? Well, Mr. Arner, if you have to leave before I get back, I will be sure to call you." He then turned and started heading slowly toward the door, writing something in his notebook.

Kassie was shocked and blurted out, "Heyyy, but I wanted… to…talk…with…you…," her voice trailing off as she finished.

The doctor had stopped in the doorway, and as he turned around slowly, he questioningly looked at Kassie who, of course, had donned her best pouty face with a big frown, and her chin tucked into her chest, while her eyes shyly looked up at him. The doctor slowly began walking back into the room. He spoke loudly, in part to keep up appearances and in part to make sure that Kassie could hear and understand what he was saying, "So who was it that said it wasn't fair that I always started at the other end of the hallway?"

Kassie winced ever so slightly and demurely confessed it was her.

The doctor said that he thought so as he nodded his head slowly up and down, and a big smile crept onto his face. He asked, "So now that you have me here before anyone else has seen me, what is it that is so important?"

"So, how am I doing?" Kassie sheepishly asked.

The doctor chuckled openly, then went into a huge production about how well she was doing, how happy the teacher was that Kassie was finally in her class, and that the rest of the kids really like her a lot. He then explained how the therapy specialists told him that she was ahead of schedule in her progress.

Kassie's face burst with excitement and quickly explained she would be going to school every day except she had therapy during that time and then needed to rest afterwards; then without even taking a breath asked if that meant she could go home now.

"Well, let's see how you're doing with your list," the doctor said.

Of course, Kassie went through the items by heart and said that she was making real progress getting dressed by herself, and she can now get to the bathroom without hardly any assistance. She then reminded him, "You've got a good report from therapy and my teacher. I've been eating all my food, even the stuff I don't like, and I'm getting stronger and stronger every day!" With that, Kassie stopped and smiled at the doctor, feeling very proud of her accomplishments.

"Okay, that's great to hear. Let's see how your walking is doing."

Kassie wheeled her chair out to the hall, conserving her energy, locked the wheels, and stood up without any assistance. She then took about twenty steps covering about twenty feet of distance. The doctor was astounded that she had made so much progress in such a short amount of time. Of course, we didn't say anything about our private training sessions.

The doctor looked surprised. "Well, you told me you were going to do better, and you certainly did. I am very proud of your progress and your desire to get well." Then he concluded, "Kassie, you are really doing far better than anyone expected."

I was following her in the wheelchair and fought the urge to tell the doctor, "Everyone but me that is," but thought better of it.

Kassie looked up at him as she sat down. "Sooo?" she asked.

The doctor smiled down at her and said that she still had some work to do on her walking, and she still needs to build up more strength and stamina before she can go home.

While we could all tell Kassie was disappointed, she understood. As she said her good-byes and began wheeling back to her room, she looked over her shoulder and said, "Okay, I'll keep working at it."

With that, the doctor looked at me and said, "There is no doubt in my mind that she will!"

Once Kassie was out of earshot, I asked, "And how about the day pass for Sunday?"

He inhaled deeply as he ran his hands across his face and on through his hair while studying my face. As he continued to look at me, he pondered the question for a while. He finally said he would make the arrangements.

I smiled and shook his hand while telling him how much I appreciated this.

He smiled back and said getting out would probably do her good, and that it would be beneficial to see how she does out of the hospital setting.

I asked him if he would like to tell her the good news himself.

He nodded and said, "Sure."

Kassie was waiting for me to help her get into bed. Even though she could do it on her own now, she liked me to help because I would sometimes "accidentally" throw her into the bed. When the doctor and I both walked back in her room, she peered at us with an inquisitive look on her face.

The doctor began, "Kassie, you know this Sunday is Easter, right?"

Kassie acknowledged that she did.

He then asked, "What do you normally do on Easter?"

Kassie got a huge smile on her face and started explaining, "Well, first, we wake up and hunt for Easter eggs that are hidden around the house and sometimes outside, too, but we don't do that anymore because our dogs like the Easter eggs as much as we do, and they don't know they're not supposed to chew on them. Then we get all dressed up and go to church, sometimes I stay awake through the whole sermon. Then after church, we go home and re-hide the Easter eggs and hunt for them again. Then the whole family gets together for a big meal. It's so much fun."

The doctor agreed that it sounded fun, but also said it sounds like it would be very strenuous too. He then asked her, "Do you think you could go home for just Easter Day and then come back that evening?"

Kassie was shocked at the question but quickly replied that being home for Easter would be, "Gi-normous!"

He told her she would have to agree to take it easy and that when she got tired, she would have to lie down for a while. Then he earnestly asked, "Kassie, will you promise me you will do that?"

Kassie quickly agreed and gave the doctor a big hug while telling him, "Thank you, thank you, thank you!"

Before leaving her room, Kassie's doctor explained that her mommy and daddy had requested to let her go home for Easter, and the only reason this was going to happen was because of how well she was doing and how hard she was working toward getting better. However, if she were to overdo it while she was home, that it would cause her to lose ground and she would have to stay at the hospital in subacute for a longer period of time before being released.

I think he was saying it so not only Kassie would understand, but so that I would, too.

He then closed the deal by asking her very pointedly, "Kassie, do you understand these rules and their consequences if not followed?"

Kassie eagerly nodded her head while assuring the doctor that she fully understood the rules. The doctor then smiled at her, gave her a hug, told her to keep up the good work, and that he would see her again before Easter.

I finally had to head off to work. I kissed my little Kassie good-bye as she sat still in her wheelchair just long enough for a smooch from me before excitedly wheeling around the room. She literally couldn't sit still; she was so excited. The huge beaming contagious smile on her face told the story; this was going to be a great day! As I was leaving, I told her to try and not get into any trouble today while I was gone, and that I would be back after work. My words fell onto deaf ears, and as I paused and glanced back to wave good-bye, Kassie's head was back, and her eyes were closed as she wheeled her chair in a stationary circle over and over again as fast as she could. Yes, I mused, it *was* going to be a great day. I stayed in the doorway smiling, watching my little girl revel in her accomplishment of a day trip home. As her wheelchair came to an abrupt stop from her foot piece running into the bed, she opened her eyes and realized I had witnessed her celebration and giggled wildly at being busted. She wheeled over to me and gave me another kiss good-bye. I gave her a wink and spun around twice on one foot before heading out into the hallway.

She proclaimed, "Daddy, you're silly!"

To which I responded, "Nuh uh!" and shot her a big smile.

As I left her room and started down the hall, I had to fight the urge to skip to the elevator. *Oh, what the heck*, I thought, *it would probably give the nurses a good laugh!* I wondered if I even remembered how to skip as I started. From behind me, I could hear Kassie giggling at the sight as she peeked at me from around her doorway. The nurses heard me coming, keys and change jingling all the way, and had come out from around the nurses' station into the hallway. From the look on their faces, I imagined it had been a while since they had heard the thunderous footsteps of a 240-pound guy skipping. As I bounded away from Kassie's room toward the nurses' station, tears of happiness began streaming down my face. I began waving to the nurses, and their looks of trepidation turned to smiles as I began singsonging, "Kassie gets to come home for Easter! Kassie's coming home for Easter!" Drawing ever closer to the somewhat amused nurses, they continued smiling, waving, and shaking their heads while reprimanding me for causing such a disturbance with my childlike raucous behavior. As I skipped past them and on toward the elevators, I knew they must be thinking, "Now I have…truly… seen…everything!"

While I was waiting for the elevator to come, I looked back toward Kassie's room at the far end of the hallway, hoping she would still be watching, and I would be able to give one more wave good-bye. To my amazement, a lot of the other kids were making their way out into the hallway to see what all the hubbub was about. Kassie was now fully out into the hallway as I waved and blew her kisses. Again, to my amazement, everyone within view waved back, they were all smiling, all of them were giggling and laughing, and some blew kisses back at me, even the nurses.

As the elevator door closed behind me, tears were rolling down my cheeks at such velocity I couldn't keep them wiped away. My heart was beating out of my chest, and when the doors opened, I was happy to see nobody was there to catch me so full of emotion. I hurriedly made my way to the car and sat down inside with a thump. I reclined the seat back as far as it would go. I thought, *Why am I acting this way?* I had to sit there for a while before I could drive. By now, I was pretty used to driving while crying; I had even decided that someday I was going to write a song called "It's Always Raining Inside My Car," but this was different. I pondered if I could be having a nervous breakdown but decided that wasn't the case. Besides, I didn't have time for a breakdown. Kassie still needed my help.

My brain swirled around like an Oklahoma tornado knowing that many of those kids whom Kassie was making friends with were terminally ill, yet they still found a way to smile and have fun and make the most of their time being happy. I started the car and headed for work remembering, "It's going to be a great day! It's going to be a great day!"

EASTER SUNDAY

As Easter drew nearer, Kassie was now more motivated than ever, and she tirelessly worked even harder and longer than before. Without anyone's knowledge, we had become a covert team of two, acting as one. She told me she could hardly wait until I got there so we could go through our routine of extra therapy. Kassie knew that I had to be there before any of our extra therapy could be done. She wanted to go home for good, and I wanted her home as quickly as possible. Theoretically, I realized this could be a dangerous combination. I made Kassie promise me that she wouldn't do any additional training by herself. I knew that Kassie could not, and would not, be shut down once she had set her mind to doing something; so as a further precaution, I re-explained the consequences of her overdoing it. She nodded in agreement, and to my chagrin, she flashed that little smile telling me that I could trust her…kind of. Meaning that as long as she didn't actually get caught doing something that she wasn't supposed to be doing, nobody would be the wiser. I sternly looked at her and stated in no uncertain terms that I was dead serious. This immediately changed her demeanor, and I knew by the look on her face she fully understood this was not up for negotiation, nor was it going to be a "Yeah, sure, Dad, (wink, wink) I'll be sure not to do that" sort of thing. She understood there was to be no additional physical therapy unless I was there to supervise, and that was that.

Later on, Lorrie, Autam, and Stevo brought dye so they could color Easter eggs with Kassie. They also drew pictures with crayons and decorated Kassie's room for Easter. Stevo and Kassie's friends from school had sent some special Easter goodies for her also.

Sunday morning came, exactly one month and one day from the time Kassie was airlifted to Phoenix Children's Hospital. She was so very happy to be out of the hospital with her family at church and was dressed to the nines in a beautiful white dress adorned with lace, and her hair all in curls. She had been up for a couple of hours before getting to church and was already showing small signs of fatigue. I knew Kassie's first test of adherence to the rules would soon be upon us. I was hoping she would voluntarily rest when that time came.

Our kids loved going to Sunday school with Grandma and Grandpa when they were little, and we still had a cherished family tradition to spend Easter morning at my parents' church, Hillside Baptist. Brother Jerry was instrumental in getting one of the very first prayer lines started when Kassie first got sick. He had also visited Kassie, Lorrie, and me at the hospital a number of times. This morning, Brother Jerry was preaching about Easter and the resurrection, and as it was a Baptist church, he could get animated at times and wasn't beyond raising his voice occasionally to emphasize a point. He began to weave Kassie's story into his sermon about God's power and stated to all that sitting right out there among everyone was the miracle girl they had all been praying for recently. He continued by saying, "When Kassie first got to the hospital, she was given only a five percent chance of living through the night! Yet there she sits with her loving family that prayed to God for a miracle."

I swallowed hard because to this point in time, Kassie was not aware how close to death she had actually gotten. I looked over to her, hoping that she had not understood, or was not paying close attention to what Brother Jerry was saying. Maybe I would luck out, Kassie may have already fallen asleep, which was somewhat customary, but when I glanced over, she was staring directly at me with a look on her face that said I had some explaining to do.

Brother Jerry continued on, delivering a wonderful sermon as was usual, and Shirley Ann had everyone singing with enthusiasm. The power of the message took on a personal tone in my mind, and it kept reminding me just how close we had come to losing our little Kassie. I couldn't help but to cry and wipe tears away throughout the sermon. I didn't feel bad though, because I noticed everyone in our little group was doing the same thing. Along the way, Kassie was trying to continue listening, but she was running out of gas quick. She decided she needed to get a little bit more comfortable leaning against Grandma, and then Grandpa, and then back again. She had been shifting back and forth for some time trying to get comfy when Kassie finally looked up to her grandma and stated that she couldn't get to sleep with Shirley Ann singing and Brother Jerry preaching, and she wished they didn't have to be so loud.

All of us sitting within earshot quietly cracked up laughing. I made a mental note to mention to Brother Jerry that his sermons were sleep proof, even to partially deaf people. Did I mention that Kassie was a great source of entertainment to us all?

After church, as we were waiting in line to shake Brother Jerry's hand on the way out, everyone was coming over to Kassie to tell her how happy they were that she was better and giving us all hugs of encouragement, exclaiming the power of God's will. When we made it to the beginning of the line and shook Brother Jerry's hand, he took extra time with Kassie. As they chatted, he made sure she knew what a wonderful family she had, and the strength that was shown in the time of crisis was inspiring. Brother Jerry's words brought tears to Kassie's eyes. She gave him a big hug and told him she knew she had a great family, then gave him a big hug again and held it a bit longer this time. As I came up to him, he grabbed my hand and pulled me close. He whispered to me what a special thing we had all witnessed, something that very few get to experience in a lifetime, and he praised God for Kassie's recovery. He then looked at me, and we had a conversation with our eyes; no words were spoken, and I gave him a big hug, too. I gathered myself and went outside where everyone was waiting. Kassie and Stevo excitedly informed me we had to go; it was time to go hunt Easter eggs.

Easter—family picture

Kassie gets a day-pass out of
Sub Acute to go to church

Autam, Kassie, and Stevo
going to Easter services at
Hillside Baptist Church

Family at hospital park—PCH 1998

Kassie and Caren-Grama Nelson

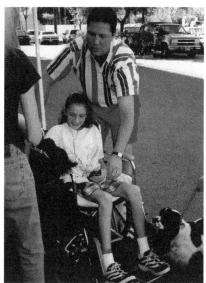

Dad, Kassie, Splash, Annie,
and Autam visit to park at
hospital with family dogs

Stevo taking Kassie for a walk with Grandpa Arner

So off we went. We were just one big happy family, enjoying each other, cutting up, and messing around. There was no emergency, there was no hospital, and there was no life-threatening illness. There was just this happy bliss that we were all together, in our world where families enjoy hanging out together, friends play with each other, and good times are had by all. None of us thought about the fact that Kassie would be returning to Sub Acute all too soon. It wasn't important; we were enjoying the time we had together, and not one second was to be wasted. Besides, I had Easter eggs to hide… and re-hide…and re-hide. There was no doubt in my mind those eggs were going to be worn out by the end of the day!

*****

When we got home, everyone changed out of their Sunday "go to church" clothes into attire that was more comfortable but still looked very nice. Kassie was pretty whipped, so we opted to hide the Easter eggs after a quick power nap. I was happy to see she was going to obey the rules, even if Easter eggs were involved. As full of energy as Kassie had always been, when she got tired, there was a very short fuse until she was asleep. This was no different in Kassie's current condition, except for now she wore out more quickly of course.

We always joked that Kassie could fall asleep on a sharp rock, because when her light switch gets pushed, she's out, no matter where she is. We have pictures of her when she was little sleeping in her highchair, or draped over her crib with her arms and head hanging out. Then as she got a bit older, we would find her asleep in interesting places like while she was at the dinner table, or halfway up the stairs on her way to bed, or on her potty chair, or dangling off the arm of the couch.

One time, when Kassie was three years old, I looked all over the house trying to find her and was becoming worried that she had gotten outside without me knowing about it, only to find her sleeping inside the cushions of the sofa. Apparently, she was searching for some Cheerios that had been dropped. I knew this because she still had a couple in her hand and was even holding one in her fingertips next to her mouth ready to pop it in. Did I mention that Kassie was a great source of entertainment for us all?

When Kassie awoke from her power nap, all the Easter eggs were hidden, and she got to search for them all by herself because Autam and Stevo had already "accidentally" found the first group of hidden eggs. Stevo took great joy in telling Kassie whether she was hot or cold in her solo search for the hidden Easter eggs. Once they were all found, Stevo and Kassie had to go back to their rooms and wait for them to be re-hid. Autam decided she was too old to hunt for "re-hid" Easter eggs, so she helped Lorrie and me hide them. Then with a holler down the hallway, out the chute they came like wild horses running down a mountain pass. Well, actually, Stevo came thundering down the hall, while Kassie very cautiously came as quickly as she could. Lorrie and I just stood there with wide smiles on our faces, holding onto each other in a loving embrace, while Autam did her best to corral Stevo from starting before Kassie got there, and then to keep Kassie from finding the easier ones before Stevo saw them. As was the tradition, Stevo and Kassie found Easter eggs as quickly as they could, and then they both counted the eggs in their baskets to make sure they had found them all, and of course to see who had found the most. Somehow or another, there were two missing, so Autam helped them find the remaining two Easter eggs by taking a turn at telling them if they were hot or cold. Miraculously, they each found one, although the elusive eggs somehow seemed to move whenever they got close. Finally, they had them cornered; Kassie found hers in my left pants pocket, Stevo found his in my right pants pocket.

It was then time to re-hide them, so off Kassie and Stevo went down the hall into seclusion until they were called on to find the freshly hidden Easter eggs again. We would laugh out loud hearing the raucousness that was coming from the end of the hallway as we re-hid the Easter eggs; only heaven knows what Stevo and Kassie were doing while they were waiting to come and find the re-hidden eggs, but whatever it was, they were having fun doing it. This went on a couple more times until we finally had to stop because we were already late in getting over to Grandma and Grandpa Arner's for Easter dinner. As we were loading up in the car, they all had their Easter baskets filled with goodies. I asked them if they thought it was a good idea to take all their candy with them, and maybe it would be better to just take a little bit instead. Amazingly, none of them thought that was a very good idea at all. Autam finalized the decision and declared, "Uncle Steve will be there, and he will want us to share with him." I smirked at them and shook my head as I continued loading everything in the car...baskets full of candy and all.

When we arrived at my parents for dinner, everyone was already there, and there was electricity in the air when Kassie walked in. You would have thought a professional athlete or a movie star was there. I looked to see if Autam and Stevo were feeling left out, but they reveled in the attention that was being thrown toward Kassie, and I immediately felt a huge sense of pride that Autam and Stevo were also happy that Kassie was home, even if she was getting the lion's share of attention at that moment. Kassie was getting huge hugs from everyone, and she was thanking them all and telling them she will be coming home for good soon. Stevo and Autam were following behind in the procession getting big hugs, too. It was a joyous occasion, and I thought, *Thank you, God, for my family and for giving Kassie back to us.*

Easter day was absolutely wonderful. We couldn't have asked for anything better. Friends and family continued to show up throughout the day to say hi and get a quick visit in with Kassie. Kassie held to her word with the doctor and did not overexert herself. When she would feel it necessary to rest, she would go and sit down or lie on Grandpa for a little while, then reemerge to the festivities with all her spunk and frivolity. As the day came to a close, there were more big hugs and kisses as we left. There was no whining or sniveling from Kassie about having to leave, just a renewed dedication to getting home as quickly as possible. She happily went back to the Sub Acute unit at Phoenix Children's Hospital, excited about her brief excursion to the real world. She slept most of the way to PCH and woke up as we arrived back at the hospital.

As we got out of the car, Kassie said, "I'll show them what it means to work hard! I'm getting out of here soon! You wait and see!" We got Kassie settled back into her room. She laid out her clothes for the next day and got everything ready she would need. Lorrie and I could tell she was excited with renewed dedication. I was happy we were right about getting her away from the hospital, if even for just one day, it was certainly advantageous. It also proved that as hell-bent as Kassie was to get out, she was willing to play by the rules set forth to her in order to achieve her goal. She had not overexerted herself, and she realized there was more work to be done before she could leave. All in all, I felt the day was a huge success and rewarded Kassie for keeping her promise to the doctor by "accidentally" throwing her into the bed.

ONE HUNDRED STEPS

W hile I was at work the following day, I got a phone call from Kassie's therapy specialists. They said that both the Occupational and Physical Therapy departments had met, and they are in agreement they could step up their regimen for Kassie's therapy. Kassie asked them to call me and make sure I was aware that she was doing so well, and that it would be okay to e-mail everyone at Shea Homes to let them know of her progress. I chuckled to myself at the request. I could tell Lorrie was down there and could hear her in the background telling Kassie to be careful, as Kassie bounced off the balancing ball hard onto the floor. As I had been working with a customer when the call came in, I thanked them for calling me from therapy and asked them to let Kassie know I was very proud of her accomplishment, but to please let her know I was working with some people right then, and I would have to talk with her a bit later. My customers asked what that was all about, so I had to give them the *Reader's Digest* version of everything, while still trying to keep their needs and desire to purchase a home in the forefront.

I always tried to call Kassie a couple of times a day when I was working to see how things were going, but some days I would be extremely busy and unable to do so. I always knew I was going to be in for it when I finally did get down there. There would be a lot of catching up to do, and Kassie liked me to know everything that went on.

As Kassie got stronger and began to do the things necessary in order for her to leave, she became increasingly persistent in asking if she was able to go home. I finally just had to tell her that if she was going to get to go home, she would need to absolutely blow their socks off. I then devised a plan to do exactly that over the next few weeks.

We continued diligently working beyond the doctor's expectations in regard to Kassie's therapy. The real final obstacle was her ability to walk the length of the hallway in one hundred steps or less; everything else was subjective.

As we approached the weekend of the seventh week at Phoenix Children's Hospital, I went around to each of the staff necessary to sign off on her individual tasks that needed to be accomplished.

1. You have to be able to dress yourself without any help.
2. You have to be able to go to the bathroom without anyone helping you.
3. You have to get released from your physical and occupational therapy specialists.
4. You have to start going to the hospital school and have the teacher agree it's okay for you to resume studies on your own.
5. You have to continue to eat enough food to make you strong enough to resume normal activities at home.
6. And lastly, you have to walk the length of the hallway to the nurses' station in less than one hundred steps…without assistance and without stopping.

I went to the head nurse to see if there was anything she was in charge of still pending from Kassie's list. Both items in her charge were easily signed off by the nursing staff. Number one and number two, good to go.

Next, I went to the therapy specialists and found out they felt Kassie was strong enough to do her daily activities without assistance. Number three, good to go.

I then visited the teacher to see how Kassie had been progressing. She felt confident that Kassie could resume her normal schoolwork, albeit that it would need to be done from home because she felt it would be too overwhelming to go to school all day. I asked if that was within the parameters discussed and if she felt Kassie was ready to leave Sub Acute and go home. She agreed that would be fine from a learning standpoint, but made sure I understood the medical part of the equation was not something she could speak for. Even though Kassie had only limited time with the hospital's teacher, she could tell Kassie was dedicated to catching up on her missed schoolwork. Number four, good to go.

Finally, I requested to speak with Kassie's nutritionist. In speaking with her, there was no question that Kassie had been eating properly, and her weight had been increasing slowly but steadily since her arrival in Sub Acute. I asked if she felt there would be any issue with Kassie going home and maintaining her strength. She felt Kassie was doing fine, and going home would pose no problems from a nutritional standpoint. Number five, good to go.

That left only the walking endurance test. We were going to have to get past this if we were to have a chance of her coming home, and we both knew it. A lot had happened in the seven weeks since Kassie had gotten sick, but in the three weeks that Kassie had been in Sub Acute, she had made unbelievable progress. This was partially due to the therapy, partially due to our covert efforts to get Kassie stronger more quickly, but mostly due to Kassie's wonderful attitude and unyielding pursuit to get well and get out of the hospital.

I asked each of the people I had spoken with to relay our conversation to the doctor. Since it was Friday, I knew we wouldn't be seeing him again until Monday, so that gave us the weekend to fine-tune our efforts and set my plan in motion. Needless to say, our weekend was busy prepping Kassie for the endurance test.

*****

When Monday finally arrived, I went down to the nurses' station and put in a request for them to page the doctor because I wanted to talk to him. I told them it was important, and I wanted to speak with him in private before he saw Kassie. I requested that they call me when the doctor got in, then asked to have him stay at the nurses' station, and I would come down to speak with him there. They said they understood, and I went back to Kassie's room to get her ready. Not too much later, the phone rang, and I was informed the doctor was at the nurses' station. Kassie and I high-fived each other, and off I went to meet with the doctor.

I arrived at the nurses' station and thanked the nurse who called me. The doctor was speaking with one of the other nurses, so I stood there patiently, first standing on one foot, and then the other as he finished up his conversation. When he finished, we exchanged pleasantries for a moment and talked about his weekend away. I then asked if he had any idea why I asked to meet with him. He said he felt pretty confident he did but invited me to lay it out for him anyway.

"First of all," I said, "I want to thank you for the excellent care that has been given since Kassie got to PCH and to Sub Acute. Kassie is almost intolerable with her desire to check out of the hospital. As you probably already know, we have pretty much gotten everyone's blessing that Kassie is ready to come home. Have you had the opportunity to talk with PT, OT, the nutritionist, the teacher, and the head nurse that I spoke with on Friday?"

The doctor acknowledged that he had received the reports from all concerned that morning and was going over everything when he received the page to come to the nurses' station.

I told him I was relieved that all the info had gotten to him, and he had a chance to review it. He then stated that even though the reports were glowing regarding Kassie's progress, he still couldn't authorize her release until she could perform the endurance test to his satisfaction, and based on her last test with him, he just couldn't see her being ready for at least a little while longer.

"I was kind of afraid you would say that," I replied. "Kassie is so determined to go home she can barely stand it, but just so I'm clear, from what you have been told, everything else is good to go?"

He acknowledged that was correct, and I continued, "So as far as you are concerned, the only thing left to accomplish is Kassie's endurance test?"

Again, he acknowledged that was correct and added that we shouldn't feel badly that Kassie hasn't passed that part of her therapy yet, because that is by far the most difficult. He reminded me that because of Kassie's condition when she got to Sub Acute, we knew it was going to take a while for her muscles to get into good enough shape for her to accomplish that challenge.

I then asked, "Doc, if you don't mind, could you please remind me what it is that Kassie needs to do for you to feel comfortable with signing off on her release?"

"Kassie will need to walk the length of the hallway to the nurses' station in no less than one hundred steps," he reiterated.

"Without assistance and without stopping, right?" I probed.

He agreed and then added, "And now that she has been signed off on all of the other items on her checklist, we will really gear our efforts to getting her strength and endurance to a point where she will be able to accomplish that. I think within a couple more weeks, she should have enough stamina to get out of here." He finished by stating, "I am very pleased with the progress that has been achieved. It is really quite amazing she has done as much as she has in the short amount of time she has been here."

I agreed, nodding my head and stating, "You know, Doc, there is no denying that Kassie has shown great work ethic, but again, just so I am clear, once Kassie meets or exceeds your expectations in the endurance test of walking the length of the hallway in one hundred steps, there wouldn't be anything else holding you from releasing her?"

"Nope," he said, "that's the last thing."

I let him know I was going to relay that info to Kassie and asked him for one final confirmation that there wasn't anything else necessary for Kassie to do other than the endurance test. He chuckled and shook his head slightly, again reaffirming that there wasn't anything else.

I thanked him for meeting with me and for him clearing up the questions in my mind on how Kassie could accomplish being released. I then asked if he would like to check on Kassie's progress while he was here.

"Sure!" he said.

As he turned to walk toward Kassie's room, I held out my hand and said, "Hold on! You just wait right here." Then I laughingly added, "You're so impatient sometimes."

He looked at me with questioning eyes, not sure what to make of what was going on.

"Just lean back and enjoy the show," I said. "I'll bring Kassie to you."

With that, I motioned to the end of the corridor where Kassie had been peeking around the corner and gestured for her to come out. I then turned my back to her and faced the doctor exclaiming, "For everyone's pleasure and enjoyment, I would like to present Kassie Arner!"

I watched as his facial expression changed from questioning to *astonishment*. As I turned to look down the hallway toward Kassie's room, you could clearly see she was decked out in full sports attire down to her running shoes. We all watched as Kassie took a few large steps, then paused with a surprised look on her face, placing her finger to her cheek and twisting it back and forth while flashing that beautiful smile from ear to ear as she broke into a jog toward us.

I thought, *What a ham, she ad-libbed the finger and cheek thing.*

I began clapping and glanced back over my shoulder gesturing for the doctor and nurses to join me, which they did. Yeah, I know, it was hopelessly corny to get them to clap, too, but I was on a mission!

Kassie jogged up to the doctor, gave him a hug, and then came to my side. She still had that huge smile on her face. As I looked down at her, my mind jumped to the thousands of times I had seen that same smiling face, and I thought to myself the only thing missing was her smacking gum and blowing a bubble. DANG IT! I should have given her a piece of gum to chew on, why didn't I think of that before! Oh well, too late now.

The doctor was shaking his head as he looked at Kassie, who was breathing a little hard, but not much. He finally said, "Kassie, you truly are extraordinary. How did you do that?"

Kassie looked up at me and gave me a wink, then casually said, "Oh, I don't know, Doc, must have been magic." Then she smiled and asked, "By the way, did you happen to count the steps? I could do it again if you forgot to count."

He said that wouldn't be necessary as he pressed on her nose with his finger.

I asked the doctor if he needed Kassie for anything else. He said he didn't, so I sent Kassie jogging back to her room, but not before Kassie asked the doctor if she was going home now.

The doctor told Kassie he would be talking with her dad about it, and that he would be down to see her after a while.

As we watched Kassie jog away, I was smiling knowing my plan had been successful and couldn't have gone any better. When I turned to face the doctor, he was already looking at me.

"You totally worked me," he stated.

I apologized and admitted my guilt. "Doc, you gotta understand, Kassie needs to get out of here. It is driving her crazy, and for her to get to the next level, she needs to be home. We have accomplished the tasks that you set for her, and she did them exceedingly well, albeit quicker than expected. I just couldn't stand telling her she had to stay in the hospital anymore."

He shot me a half smile and nodded that he understood my dilemma.

I then repeated Kassie's question, "So does this mean Kassie is going home today?"

He looked at me and said, "I'll start the paperwork. There will need to be some sign-offs from a few additional people that should be able to see her today. If all goes well, Kassie could be released in the morning."

I jumped for joy and shook his hand, which brought a yelp from the end of the hallway where Kassie had been peeking from her doorway. I thanked him again and shook each of the nurse's hands as I quickly scurried down the hallway to Kassie's room. Kassie was hopping up and down when I got there, and we hugged each other tight.

"I better get packing," she said. "Will you help me before you bring the car around?"

I laughed and told Kassie we couldn't leave right this second. There was some paperwork that needed to be completed, and a few people still had to see her and sign off on her going home.

Kassie looked shocked and said, "What do you mean we can't go? I did what I was supposed to do and even more, didn't I?"

I agreed she had exceeded her necessary requirements, but that didn't mean she could pack up and leave. "There are some things that have to be done before anyone can be released from the hospital. Everything should be done today though, and you will get released sometime tomorrow."

Kassie began to pout and quietly said, "I want to go home today, Daddy. I don't want to wait until tomorrow."

I shook my head at her. "Sorry, baby, we can't rush this. The best it's going to be is tomorrow, but that gives you plenty of time to tell your new friends here good-bye, okay?"

With that, she nodded her head, and I said, "Why don't you give your mom a call and tell her everything that happened this morning? She will be happy to know you are coming home."

Kassie literally wiped away her pouty face with her hand and smiled, regaining the previous happiness and excitement, then pounced on the bed and grabbed for the phone. As she dialed home, she said to me, "I guess I'll have to wait until tomorrow to start training for field day." Then with an astonished look on her face, she yelled, "Mommy! Guess what!"

MAY 11

All sorts of specialists, nurses, and doctors filtered in and out of Kassie's room that day. Most of them didn't stay long or do much more than say good-bye, telling her what a wonderful girl she was and wishing her the best. Kassie enjoyed speaking with each and every one of them. She thanked them for all they had done for her, and that she wouldn't forget how hard everyone had worked on her behalf. I had called the fourth floor to thank them one last time and to have them spread the word to everyone that Kassie was going home. Some of the people from the fourth floor came by on their breaks to wish Kassie well. Those visits were a bit more tearful though on everyone's part, and it was obvious that Kassie would always be someone special to them. To those who had worked with her and seen her go from only having a 5 percent chance of living through the night to being the Miracle Girl on Four, she would always be a part of them; every bit as much as each one of them would always hold a special place in our hearts. Some even told me that patients like Kassie are why they do what they do. They were part of something bigger than the sum of the parts, and it gave them purpose.

We had been through the war together, and we had survived. We had witnessed miracles together, and we were awed by the power and unwavering love of God. I knew that although time passes, my appreciation of these people would never falter, and my remembrance of the many who prayed and put their lives on hold on Kassie's behalf would never dim.

How could a place we so wanted to leave be held in such high regard? I pondered. In some weird way, the hospital had a feeling of *home*, and the people who worked here felt like *family*. I knew in my soul that from here on out, anything I could do to help PCH, I would do wholeheartedly. I was Phoenix Children's Hospital's greatest fan.

I had barely finished that thought when the Miracle Network for PCH asked if they could do an interview before Kassie left. They said it would air on their next telethon. I asked Kassie what she thought, and we happily agreed to spread the word about the great work they were doing here. Kassie was dressed in her going home clothes and had her softball glove there. Another part of her covert training we had secretly been working on for a couple of weeks was to get her throwing arm back in shape. The Miracle Network thought that would be cool to show so they had Kassie throw a few tosses to me in the room. They also said they would like to do a follow-up at home a bit later to finish the segment once Kassie got settled. This sounded good to me, and Kassie agreed; anything we could do to help the cause was fine by us.

When we moved from the fourth floor, we had packaged up most of the cards, pictures, and stuffed animals, because we knew the room on the eighth floor was going to be much smaller. Once we got everything off the walls from her room on the fourth floor, I had been amazed at how different the room looked. It didn't feel like Kassie's room anymore. The nurses asked if it would be okay to leave the window painted for a while. One of them quipped they didn't think they would be able to go cold turkey from Kassie.

We had only brought over her favorite things to the new room at Sub Acute. I couldn't believe we still had two large boxes of stuff when we packed Kassie up to go home for good. She carried the soft oversized bunny rabbit that Lisa Saba and Bette Knoell from Shea Homes had given her; that wasn't allowed to go into a box. The helium-filled, life-sized Elmo balloon that was dropped off by Coach Charlie from the team had its own place of honor, and it was soon to enjoy its ride home in my back seat.

As I continued to load up the car with Kassie's recent life, it was hard to fathom we were actually leaving the hospital, exactly two months to the day of her arrival. I have to admit, I was experiencing a bit of bittersweet trepidation. As I was loading the boxes into the car, I was thinking about what the neurologist, Dr. Bernes, said during his final visit. While he was very happy with Kassie's outcome, he told us in private that there was a chance that Kassie could experience night terrors. He said that many people who had been in a coma or had near-death experiences will awake in the night in a cold sweat, shaking and shivering from a dream they had. It would seem more vivid and real than any other nightmare that Kassie had ever experienced, and that we needed to be ready to meet that head on if they were to occur. He had us set an appointment for a month later for Kassie to come and meet with him.

Just then, Elmo began to fly away, and I snapped back to reality. I snatched multiple times at the string that had come untied from one of the boxes I had just set down on the trunk of the car. I made one last attempt at grabbing it by stepping onto the bumper for one final leap of desperation, but alas, it was to no avail. I realized Elmo was going on a long trip somewhere other than our house. I watched Elmo drift off to obscurity, up, up, and over the hospital, never to see Kassie again. I immediately wondered where I could go on such short notice to hide my crime but decided it wouldn't be the same. I would just have to deal with the consequences of my daydreaming while I should have been vigilant to Elmo. When I told Kassie that Elmo wouldn't be making the trip home with us and that he had escaped, Kassie looked at me a bit disappointed but didn't give me any grief about it. She was happy to be going home, and she wasn't about to let anything rain on her parade...not even an AWOL Elmo!

FROM HOMECOMING TO HOME PLATE

Over the next couple of days, we all settled into the routine of having Kassie back home. For the most part, Kassie was self-sufficient and didn't require anything extra from us other than time. She wasn't as fast at getting ready as she used to be, and she did still tire more quickly than normal, but other than that, all was good. I got in touch with the school, and they handled everything in regard to providing a home school teacher. I met with the administrators at Moon Mountain to determine what would be necessary for Kassie to graduate with her class. I was hopeful that Kassie would not need to be held back a year, and the administration said as long as Kassie was able to complete her schooling from home and the home teacher felt she was ready to advance, she would be able to.

I wanted to get Kassie back into the swing of things and get her life back to normal as soon as possible. Lorrie had concerns about pushing her too fast and wanted to have her take a less aggressive approach of rest and relaxation to allow her body to recover. In all honesty, this caused a pretty serious debate between us, and it was decided to consult her doctors as to the best approach.

The kids had all gotten home from school and were out in the front yard with a few of the neighboring kids shooting some hoops, rollerblading, and generally just hanging out. Kassie was enjoying her first day back home from the hospital and was practicing for the upcoming field day. While Kassie had certainly taught herself to walk again, and could even do a casual jog pretty well, she was all out of sorts when it came to running. She had come into the house to get me to help her train for field day and said she just didn't feel right when she ran. So out the door we went.

Tommy and Trent Tewers were out front playing. Trent and Stevo were best friends and played on my football team with Cody Wilt. The Tewers were a family of four boys, all very athletic, all very competitive, and all very much boys. Their parents, Kevin and Julie, were very involved in sports, and our families immediately hit it off. Trent was the youngest of the four and a year older than Stevo. This was an eye-opening friendship for Stevo, who grew up in a family of girls. The life of roughhousing, wrestling, and getting pounded on by his surrogate big brothers helped to mold Stevo into a "real" boy, as he called it. He liked hanging out with the Tewers, and they enjoyed having a new guy around to play with and pound on. It took Stevo a little bit, but soon he was giving as good as he got…kind of. Stevo became somewhat of a fixture at the Tewers's household, and if Stevo wasn't at their house, Tommy and Trent were at ours. Tommy was Kassie's age, and because they were all so close in age, the four of them hung out together quite a bit. Tommy and Trent were impressed with Kassie's athleticism. They respected her ability in sports and admired her speed. So as I stood out there watching Kassie's body fight with itself, trying to get everything to work at the same time, my heart was heavy knowing that Kassie had a huge amount of work ahead of her. Her body had lost its memory on how to run. Her muscles were now ill-suited to complete the task she had previously performed effortlessly. Just a couple of months before, Kassie had rocketed around the bases with breakneck speed, as if she were skating on glass. Where before, it seemed Kassie had the grace of a gazelle, she now looked as though her body didn't know which way to run. Her arms and legs were out of sync and where once there was a symphony playing in rhythm as she ran, there were now three garage bands playing different songs as loud as possible at the same time.

I wanted to create a baseline, so we marked off the fifty yards and timed Kassie as she ran it. She completed it in just over ten seconds. Kassie scoffed and said I had made a mistake and started walking back to do it again when I stopped her and told her there was no mistake. She was out of breath and sweating as she turned to me.

She asked quietly, "Are you sure, Daddy? That's over four seconds slower than I can run."

I nodded my head that I was sure and had her come and rest. As she rested up, we talked. "Listen, honey," I told her, "there are a lot of training techniques we can use to get you back to where you were, but it's not going to happen overnight. As a matter of fact, this is going to be a long haul to get your physique and stamina to a point where your body is working together. I have a call in to the doctors to find out how much exercise you should be doing, and once we find out what their opinion is, we will do that."

"*Or more*," Kassie added with a very determined look on her face and an even more determined tone to her voice.

I continued, "Well, Kassie, we also want to make sure that we don't overdo it," remembering Lorrie's concerns, as well as the warning of the doctor when Kassie came home for Easter.

"Dad, that's BS," Kassie argued. "I'm in a lot better shape now than I was, and I need to get started on getting back to being me! You know me better than any doctor does! C'mon, let's get started!" And with that, off she walked toward the starting line where she had previously been training.

We went back to the basics; walking with high knees and thrusting opposite elbows, practicing to bounce up off her toes, as she skipped in this fashion. Instead of practicing in the fifty-yard marked off area, we marked off ten yards and practiced high skipping. As she began working out, I walked over to where Tommy and Trent were. I felt certain they had heard the earlier exchange between us and went over to explain what was going on. They had been watching Kassie, and I could tell they were at a loss as to why Kassie wasn't herself, why she looked so funny when she ran, and why her outward appearance had changed so much. While Kassie had some tone back to her muscles, she was still skin and bones, not a skeleton any longer, but skin and bones all the same. She also had a hollow and feeble look to her, like she was malnourished.

I stood next to the boys for a bit and then said, "You know, boys, Kassie's been through a lot, and she's doing her best to get back into shape, but it's going to take some time. I would appreciate it if you wouldn't make fun of her. I know she looks a little bit goofy when she tries to run and—" Tommy cut me off mid-sentence with the look he shot me.

"We would never do anything to hurt Kassie," Tommy said, his voice full of conviction.

Then Trent added, "Yeah, Coach, we want Kassie to get better, and we'll do everything we can to help."

My heart exploded, and I felt tears begin to well up. I felt ashamed that I would think that just because these guys were kids, and kids do mean things sometimes without thinking first, that they would say something mean to Kassie. I patted them on the shoulder and barely got out, "Thanks, guys!" before hastily retreating to the house to hide my emotions. I should have known they would be there for Kassie, why would I have thought anything else from them? The boys held true to their word without exception, and at times, they *vigorously* made sure nobody else made fun of, or kidded Kassie either.

*****

The doctor called the next day. I told him about my discussion with Lorrie regarding how much exercise Kassie should be getting and where to draw the line on what is too much.

He was somewhat ambiguous in his response by saying, "Whatever Kassie feels she is up for is probably going to be all right, just don't let her overdo it."

I explained that was like saying, "If you want to blow something up, go ahead and do it, just don't use too much dynamite!" If it was left up to Kassie, all she would be doing is training, exercising, and getting back into top shape. When she is driven about something, she's like the Energizer Bunny, she keeps going and going and going.

I described what I wanted to do and asked for his opinion. I told him we were currently training so Kassie could compete in her school's field day in about a month. I also told him I thought it would be a good idea to have Kassie rejoin her softball team and wondered if they could prescribe some physical therapy at the sports rehab center that was close by.

The doctor agreed it would be fine to have her do that and warned to just make sure that Kassie's not getting too exhausted while doing those activities. I thanked him for calling and let him know that Lorrie would probably want to talk with him as well, just to verify I fully understood what he had told me and to make sure he fully understood what Kassie and I wanted to do. He laughed and said he understood, but the more we could get Kassie into her normal routine, the better it would be for her. He wanted her recovery to take as little time as possible so her muscles wouldn't lose any more memory than they already had.

When I told Lorrie what the doctor had said, she quizzed me pretty good on what I asked and what his response was. She also made sure that I said this or that and made sure he understood about this or that.

I assured her I had told him exactly what I wanted to do, and he told me it would be okay. I told her to call if it would make her feel better, and I assured Lorrie that I wouldn't do anything that would hurt Kassie. I had truly, fully explained what I wanted to do, and the doc said okay.

With that, she begrudgingly okayed it but said she didn't like it.

Lorrie wanted the best for Kassie, as did I. We just had different ways of getting to the same place...after all, Lorrie is left-handed, which is my go-to answer for anything and everything when we disagreed about something. Lorrie also knew that I sometimes hear what I want to hear, especially if it's something I feel strongly about. I was happy that Lorrie was willing to take the doctor's advice over her own wishes, and I made sure that Kassie was aware that Mom was allowing her to do those things even though she had reservations about it, so it would be a good idea for her to thank her mom for allowing it. We continued practicing, and Kassie continued working hard to find her stride.

I called Coach Charlie and asked how he felt about having Kassie rejoin the team.

He agreed without hesitation and said the girls would be excited to have her back.

I reminded him that Kassie wasn't the same athlete as before, and that she still didn't realize that she can't do what she had always just done on reflex before she got sick.

Coach Charlie said he didn't care about any of that; he just wanted her back on the team. He added, "Besides, it's perfect timing. It's the final game of the season. It just wouldn't be right if she didn't play in at least one game." We both laughed, and I told him we would see him at the game.

The following day, the *Arizona Republic* newspaper called and wanted to know if it would be all right to do a story on Kassie. They had heard from somebody at the hospital about the Miracle Girl on Four, and the newspaper wanted to run Kassie's story on the front page of the paper.

I was flabbergasted at the thought. I explained that if it would be beneficial for PCH, and it would give people insight that miracles do still happen, then we would be all for it, but I would need to check with Kassie and her mother first. If it was okay with them, I would call back tomorrow and authorize it.

They said that would be fine, and they looked forward to meeting Kassie.

When we talked about it that night at the dinner table, we discussed the pros and cons of it. It would mean that we could get Kassie's story out, which could be very uplifting to many. It would also give some great publicity to PCH, which all of us agreed would be great. However, it would also mean that we would have to relive some of the darkest moments of our lives and dredge up feelings that we were all trying to put behind us. It was also possible this could be a disruption to our lives, and that these things sometimes take on a life of their own. There may also be people who want to see or get close to the miracle girl, and that could bring up a whole new set of problems and possibilities. But in the final analysis, we determined there would be more good to come of it than there were possibilities for the bad. I was happy to spread the word about the miracles that had given Kassie back to us and to give PCH some well-deserved credit. Even more than that, I was proud of Kassie and wanted her to realize something positive from the dedication and hard work that she had put into her recovery.

When I called the *Arizona Republic* back the following morning, they were excited that we accepted their invitation to be interviewed. We began trying to set up the best time for everyone including the photographer, and it was determined that the best time would be in the evening. The only evening possible for them was the same night of Kassie's softball game. I asked if it would be okay to do it the following week, but they thought it would be a great idea to go to the game. I said fine, and the date was set.

*****

While we were at PCH, we learned that many of the nurses had played sports when they were younger, and some even still played on leagues. They had said they would like to come out to see one of Kassie's games sometime, so I called PCH and let them know that Kassie was going to play in a softball game next week, and if they wanted to come and watch, they were welcome.

Game day arrived, and the interview went well. The reporter and photographer werc at the game talking to the people in the stands, and us, and the people from PCH who had come.

It was a tight game, and the team we were playing was the first-place team. We were the home team and were getting our final bats in the last inning. We were down by two runs, and there was one out with a runner on second when Kassie came up to bat. There was electricity in our stands with anticipation that Kassie would do something to help the team. Parents and fans were chanting, "Speedy… Speedy… Speedy," when the pitcher threw the first pitch. Whiff! Strike one. Kassie kicked the dirt with her back foot and dug in, the pitcher looked for the sign, and all the while, the chanting continued from the stands, "Speedy… Speedy… Speedy." Then the next pitch was on its way. Crack! The ball rocketed off the bat between first and

THE ARIZONA RE

© Copyright 1998, The Arizona Republic

...rday, May 30, 1998   ★★   Phoenix, Arizona   www.azcentral.com

Playing with heart

'Miracle girl' beats odds of survival

By Jennifer Barrett
The Arizona Republic

Kassie Arner didn't know how close she'd come to dying until Easter morning.

"The pastor said, 'Here's the girl that had a 5-percent chance of living,' and everyone was just floored," said her mom, Lorrie. "Kassie just looked up at her dad like he had a lot of explaining to do."

Even now, six weeks after the 11-year-old Phoenix girl was able to leave the hospital, her dad, David, is still not sure he can explain it.

What he knows is that his little girl came down with the flu, took an afternoon nap, and didn't wake up.

When they rushed Kassie to Phoenix Children's Hospital on March 11, her lips and fingers were blue, a lung had filled with fluid, and her organs had begun to shut down.

Doctors gave her a 5 percent chance of living through the night.

"I think they just didn't want to tell us she was going to die," her mom said.

More than 40 friends and family members gathered around Kassie's bed that night. Dr. David Bryda, director of the critical care unit, told the Arners that Kassie had a severe lung infection called strep pneumo. He promised her family he would keep Kassie comfortable and pain-free that night.

— Please see MIRACLE, Page A2

Michael Chow/The Arizona Republic

Her softball coach said he never expected to see her back. But Wednesday Kassie Arner joined her team for its last game of the season. She scored a run that helped her team advance to the championships.

second base into right field. The runner from second base scored on the hit, but Kassie was held to a single. Kassie had a huge smile on her face knowing she had just helped her team. She was all business though as she eyed second base, waiting for the pitch to the batter to be thrown. Kassie, Charlie, and I had talked before the game about how she wasn't as fast on the bases as she used to be, so she needed to keep that in mind. I wondered if she was keeping it in mind right now as she took off for second base as soon as the pitcher threw the ball. It seemed like only yesterday Kassie was begging for them to try and throw her out, now I was worried she was going to get picked off going to second. In came the throw from home, and Kassie dove headfirst for the bag in a cloud of dirt and dust.

"SAFE!" yelled the umpire, and the crowd went wild. I looked at Charlie and he looked at me, both of us wiping our brow. Whew, that was close. Kassie called time-out and brushed herself off, glancing in my direction with a wicked little smile on her face while she blew a bubble and popped it. I smiled back shaking my head and mouthing, "That was close."

On the next pitch, the batter hit a dribbler to third. Kassie got a good jump and made it to third, sliding in safe, but the batter was thrown out at first. There were two down with the tying run on third, Kassie. She messed with the pitcher's head acting like she was stealing home and then equally messed with the catcher trying to get her to throw it to third so she could steal home. But the catcher was good and ran her back to the bag before throwing it back to the pitcher. The count got to full, and the batter hit a pop fly between first base and right field. Kassie took off like her life depended on it and was sliding across home plate about the same time as the ball hit the ground.

The umpire behind the plate yelled, "Fair ball!" and the batter scampered past first before the throw got there. "Safe! Safe!" the umpire yelled, as he pointed at home plate and then to first base, and the crowd again erupted with cheers.

Kassie was yelling congratulations over to the runner at first base for knocking her in and tying the score. Then as Kassie got to the dugout, she got mobbed by her teammates on the bench.

Panthers softball 1998 with Kassie

Coach Charlie with the Panthers, Kassie waiting to bat

When the runner who knocked Kassie in eventually scored, everyone was rejoicing in beating the first-place team. Coach Charlie and I caught each other's eye and just smiled, shaking our heads at each other. It really was unbelievable that Kassie was an intricate part of the win, but that is exactly the way it happened.

Could you have even written a better ending? I thought. I was so thankful that Coach Charlie had allowed Kassie back onto the team and therefore to be a part of this victory. Needless to say, there would be no stopping her on her quest for complete recovery. Kassie would be more motivated now than ever, but first she would take time to celebrate this victory with her friends. The Panthers had beaten the first-place team in the final game of the year!

PRAYERS REALIZED

Our daily training had shaved two full seconds off Kassie's fifty-yard dash time, and she was beginning to get a little bit of form back in her running. Kassie worked tirelessly to get faster at the sports rehab facility. The trainers there took a keen interest in her and did everything possible to help get her strength back. Not only did she work out with weights and stretching exercises, but she also worked out at the speed and agility place next door. There Kassie was, eleven years old, working out with high school athletes, college athletes, and even pros who were there to increase their already blazing fast speed. Seeing that caliber of athlete training and working to get better energized Kassie's desire to do the same. Her trainers would constantly tell me how motivated she was, and that she has more drive than a lot of the high school kids they get in there. I also signed Autam and Stevo up for speed and agility training. It was quite a workout, but it was good having all the kids involved in the same activity at the same time. Lorrie had settled into the fact that Kassie's workout regimen was making her stronger, and she could see that she was becoming healthier every day. She worked out at least four times a week and then also trained with me when I got home. Plus, I knew she was doing extra running and skipping with the boys on our street when they were available, which was almost always. If Kassie asked, they dropped what they were doing and came a runnin'.

Kassie had been home from the hospital for about two weeks and was continuing to get stronger and stronger. I asked if she felt up to going to my sales meeting with me. I explained we have a sales meeting every Friday, and everyone there would be interested in meeting the girl whom they now knew but few had actually met.

Kassie happily agreed that she would love to go to my sales meeting. We began talking about what she would do when she got there, and she started asking if certain people were going to be there.

She asked, "Daddy, is John Ferrier going to be there, and how about Dottie, is she going to be there? How about Bette and Lisa that gave me my super soft rabbit?" Then she rattled off a few descriptions of others whom she had met while at the hospital but couldn't remember their names.

I told her yes, they would probably be there, but before we could make definite plans, I would need to get permission to have a special guest speaker. I assured her though that I thought I could get it approved.

Her eyes got wide as she realized by guest speaker that I meant her.

"Daddy," she said, "I couldn't stand in front of all those people and talk to them, what would I say?"

"Well, I guess you could tell them that you are feeling better, and that you appreciate all the cards and gifts they sent you. Then you could tell them what you are doing to get stronger. They would probably like to hear about that."

She nodded her head in agreement that she could do that, and that it wouldn't be too hard to do.

I explained to her that everyone who will be there are our friends, and there is no reason to be apprehensive about talking to them. If she starts to get butterflies in her stomach, just talk directly to someone she knows or recognizes, and that will take care of any nervousness she might have.

Kassie said she was really excited to go to the meeting because she knew that everyone there really helped in her getting well, and she wanted to say thanks.

I felt that would be a really nice gesture and called my boss at Shea Homes to get the okay. After assuring my boss that Kassie was up to the task, I got permission to have Kassie come down that Friday. They were concerned that it would be too overwhelming to have Kassie in front of that many people at one time so soon after being released. My boss reminded me that our group can be intimidating even to seasoned speakers and how at times they can even seem somewhat disinterested, but I explained how important it was to her, and he finally agreed.

Our sales meetings were pretty regimented with a timed schedule that was adhered to. On the schedule, it just stated, "Guest Speaker," and ten minutes for the time frame. Her time was slotted about a half hour into the meeting, so I had Lorrie bring Kassie to the building just before she was scheduled. That way, they could leave right after and get Kassie back to meet with her home teacher.

As the meeting progressed and it became time for Kassie to speak, they verified the guest speaker was here, which she was, and she was right outside the door in the hallway. Then they announced, "We have a very special guest speaker with us today. Normally, we have this time set aside for one of our trade partners or finance specialists to give us some information necessary to help us sell homes, but today we wanted to bring you someone that has a more personal message to give you."

Everyone was looking at each other trying to figure out if anyone knew who the speaker was, as this was very much out of the ordinary. All eyes were on the doorway when they announced, "We would like to welcome our VERY special guest to you, please welcome one of our very own family members, Kassie Arner."

Kassie smiled and waved to everyone as she walked in to meet an astonished group. She was dressed in a very colorful dress with pretty dress shoes and had spent quite a bit of time getting ready this morning with her mommy because Kassie's hair was all in bouncy curls. By the time Kassie had reached the podium, she was receiving a standing ovation. As I took my place at her side and gave her a hug for luck, I could tell that she was shocked at the reception. While she realized that everyone at Shea had really been involved with things since she became sick, she had no idea of what her appearance there meant to everyone. They were seeing the outcome to their prayers. It's one thing to know you were involved in something miraculous, but it is really quite something else to see the miracle standing before you. I decided to preface what Kassie was here for and allow her time to recover from the overwhelming applause.

"Thank you all so very much for such a warm reception," I began. "Kassie and I, as well as all of our family and friends, are very well aware of your contribution into Kassie's speedy recovery. We thought we would come down today to share a little about what Kassie's been up to since being released from the hospital and allow you to see firsthand how much better Kassie has gotten."

With that, I stepped away a few steps and allowed Kassie to speak. Kassie was nervous, but she started by saying, "Like Daddy said, I am doing a lot better, and I'm studying hard for school so I can graduate with the rest of my friends at the end of the year." Excitedly, she added, "I am training for field day, and I will try to make you all proud of me." Then she paused and said, "But what I really wanted to do…what I want to say…what I want to tell you is…" The tears welled up and began to flow. "I wanted to come here and thank you…because I know it was because of you and your prayers that I am alive right now." Then with full emotion, she exclaimed, "Thank you for saving my life!"

I was blown away. I had no idea she was going to say those things; I had no idea she felt so deeply, or had even contemplated what she said. As I quickly walked to her side again, tears were flowing from my eyes, and I was clearly choked up by Kassie's emotion. I pulled Kassie close to me, and she buried her face in my chest. As I looked out to this roomful of professionals to silently apologize for my own emotion, I noticed there wasn't a dry eye out there. Men and women alike were so moved by my little girl's confession of how she really felt. They allowed their own walls to be taken down by the sincerity of her admission.

I think people rarely have the opportunity to see what actual benefits come from prayer other than the personal good feelings you get, knowing you have done something for someone else simply because it was the right thing to do. Rarely do you get that one-on-one situation that makes you realize the magnanimous effect had on the person who was the recipient of your prayers. The truly life-changing parameters that are now eternally part of your life; the unchallengeable knowledge there is a God, and He does listen.

Slowly, people began to clap, with the realization setting in that they had just witnessed someone speak completely from her heart to them. Giving them the only thing she could offer, her sincere thanks to them for praying for someone they didn't even know personally. Soon, everyone was standing and clapping again. Initially, this made both Kassie and me cry even harder, but soon we both began smiling and going out to shake people's hands, and Kassie got huge hugs from most, if not all, of my fellow sales agents and company personnel. While Kassie had made a large impact on the lives of my friends because of her peril, she made an even larger impact because of her words. She allowed people to get a glimpse of the real Kassie; not the cute one dressed up all pretty for them with that huge contagious smile that set everyone at ease, but the real Kassie, full of sweetness and sincerity.

An even more unusual unscheduled break was called to allow everyone to compose themselves.

I walked out to the hallway with Kassie and said, "Wow, kid, that was really something. Where did that come from?"

Kassie admitted she didn't know, and that it was not what she had planned on talking about.

I gave her a big kiss and told her how proud I was of her, and that we would talk more later.

She gave me a big hug and ran off down the hallway to meet up with her mom and head home to work with the home teacher the Washington School District provided for her.

As I reentered the meeting room, some people were still visibly moved by Kassie's words and came up to tell me what it meant to them personally to see their prayers answered. Some came up and just acknowledged what a wonderful little girl I had, while still others came up to give me a hug. I suppose I looked like I needed one. I have to admit that went much differently than I anticipated, and the feelings I witnessed in that room stay with me even today.

*****

That weekend, Kassie and I went to PCH to see the doctors and nurses and to just say hi. Kassie liked going down to "her" hospital because she liked visiting the doctors and nurses on four, in Sub Acute, and Mike Sabo in, as Kassie called it, the hearing building.

As we visited with Dr. Tellez and Dr. Liu, they were excited to share with us some fantastic news. Dr. Tellez told Kassie she should be proud, because as a result of Kassie doing so well, he confidently placed an eighteen-year-old young man who weighed over two hundred pounds on ECMO that had lymphoma and failing lungs. Despite naysayers saying it wouldn't work, they were excited to share that he was alive today because of what they had learned while treating Kassie. Kassie asked if she could meet him. They agreed but were concerned it might bring back some bad memories. She assured them she would be fine, and they took her to see him.

It was interesting meeting this nice young man and his family. Although he was still very sick when Kassie was introduced to him, he knew who she was immediately. They chatted for a moment, and he told her thanks for surviving. Kassie giggled and said she didn't remember doing too much, and that it was the doctors who deserved all the credit.

I thought to myself that while that statement was true, the doctors did deserve credit, Kassie had a bigger hand in her own survival than she realized, and then of course there were those tiny insignificant pesky "miracles" we all witnessed. I smiled to myself thinking about the magnanimous events that had unfolded before us.

Later on, we found out the eighteen-year-old patient did very well and was presented at a medical conference, which generated an increased interest in using ECMO on patients with malignancies.

The interesting thing about a miracle is you never know the purpose. Is it that God has a special plan for you, or someone you come in contact with and made a difference in, or one of your future children who wouldn't have been born if you had not survived, or maybe it would be one of your great-great-great-great-grandkids that God has a plan for. Who knows, maybe the greater purpose of this miracle was for this new patient who wouldn't have survived if not for Kassie, or maybe one of his future acquaintances or children. It is said God works in mysterious ways, and while that is the case, we don't spend a whole lot of time thinking about it; we just hope we're around when it happens.

Before leaving, we walked through all the pods to see anyone there who had worked with Kassie. Everyone made a big fuss and told Kassie how much they appreciated her coming to visit them, and that it reminded them why they come to work every day. They truly treated her like a rock star.

On the way home, Kassie was quieter than normal. I asked her if everything was all right.

"Yeah…," she said, trailing off.

I knew there was something more, so I prodded. "But?"

She looked at me all perplexed and said, "Daddy, I really like it when people make a big deal out of me coming to visit, and I enjoy all the attention, but I really don't know if I am deserving of it. I didn't do anything. Everybody else did everything…right?"

As I pulled onto the freeway to head home, I told her how I felt about the situation.

"Well, sweetheart, I understand why you might feel that way, but what you are not realizing is how much you fought to survive. It's what we all witnessed in the weeks before you woke up. You don't really know what happened, but believe me, you are deserving of the admiration you receive from everyone. Do you want to know what Autam told me?" Kassie nodded her head. "She said that she thought if anyone could survive the illness you had, she felt that of our three kids, you were the one with the best chance. Because of your tenacity, and stubbornness, and your commitment to winning at all costs, you survived where the rest may not have. Trust me when I tell you, you are an inspiration to people that work within the medical field. You are a living miracle. There's not a bunch of your kind running around."

Kassie responded, "I don't feel like I'm anyone's miracle. I feel the same as I always did, just different because of being sick."

I said, "I'm glad it was God's will to give our little Kassie back to us pretty much the same way as before you got sick." Then I explained to her, "That was one of my prayers to God, to return you to us the same as before you got sick. Even though getting sick has left you with some challenges that we are working very hard to overcome, I feel that my prayer was answered. We received three miracles, I cherish every moment I have with you and whatever we have to do to get you back to the way you were is what we'll do. God has a plan, and I'm willing to follow that plan as best I can with you. It's how I will show my thanks to Him, and to you, for never giving up. Does that help you understand why people believe you're such a big deal?"

Kassie smiled and said that she supposed so.

*****

Shortly thereafter, Kassie got the news that she was going to need to be fitted for hearing aids. This news totally upset her, and she absolutely did not want to wear hearing aids.

I went down to visit my parents and told them the news about the hearing aids. Most people don't understand that hearing aids just amplify sound. They don't make things clearer or easier to understand, they simply pick up all noise indiscriminately. It doesn't matter if you are trying to hear what someone is saying if the air conditioner kicks on or there is another noise in the room, hearing aids pick up that noise and amplify it also. My dad had hearing aids that he wore some of the time. He got to where he looked at you when you spoke so he could see what you were saying. He didn't particularly care to wear his hearing aids either. Of course, they were the old kind that were large and stuck outside his ears. We were at a family gathering one time and after repeating the punch line to a joke two or three times for him, he actually said, "I can't understand what you're saying, get me my glasses." We all cracked up and from then on, we constantly ribbed him about needing his glasses to hear with.

My dad asked what kind of hearing aids she would have to wear, and I told him they were the kind that sat inside the ear. He couldn't understand why Kassie was making such a big fuss about something nobody would even notice.

I agreed it didn't make much sense to me either and that I had brought up that same argument with her myself. I said to my dad, "I even tried to reason with her by letting her know it wasn't like she was going to have to wear those earmuff-looking things like Grandpa has."

He laughed briefly, then thought about what I had said and looked perplexed while commenting, "Thanks, son!" and laughing even harder.

Field day finally came, and luckily, the new hearing aids had not arrived yet, so we averted the battle of trying to convince her to wear them on this special day. The doctor said she needed to start wearing her hearing aids as soon as they came in so she could start getting used to them.

Kassie was so excited to see her friends from school when she arrived for field day. To this point, she still had not gone back to the school for any length of time for classes. Every so often, we would go up there and talk with her teachers and get schoolwork, but that was usually after school was out.

When we got there, Kassie was again mobbed by her friends. They were all so excited their secret weapon was back because now they were sure to win; after all, Kassie always won every event she was in. This day, unbeknownst to them, she was only entered into one event though. Her only event was the fifty-yard dash—the event she had been so vigorously training for.

When the gun sounded, they all took off. Kassie was finding her stride and running with decent form. What a difference it was in the few short weeks of our training when Kassie's body didn't seem to know exactly what to do. Come to think of it, it wasn't that long ago when she couldn't even walk by herself, and here she was now competing in a race for her school.

I watched with so much pride as Kassie continued down the track with her friends in a race she had never lost. She was giving it her all. The training and pain that she had pushed through to get to this point was now coming to this one point of culmination. We were all standing and cheering as she neared the finish line. She never let up and pushed all the way through…and came in dead last. I was up in the stands hoopin' and hollerin' for my little Kassie, so very proud of her.

You could tell the people in her class were dumbfounded by the strange turn of events. She came back to the stands after sincerely congratulating the winner on a great race, a friend of hers who had raced many times against Kassie with a much different outcome. Her friends were asking what had happened to her, how come she didn't run fast, sharing with her their disappointment that she hadn't won the race. Kassie took it all in stride and told them the better runner won that day. She also shared that her illness had caused her to not be as fast as she used to be, but she was training to get faster. They offered to let her compete in some other events if she wanted to, but she declined, saying that she would rather hang out with her friends and catch up.

Kassie laughed and had a good time, cheering on her friends as they competed in events where previously she had been the hero. She gave high-fives to her friends and told them how great it was they won, or came in second, or whatever happened to be the case. Finally, it was the end of the meet, and it was time to go home. Kassie bid farewell to all of her friends. Throughout the course of the day, Kassie had been markered up with BFFs from multiple friends, although to me it looked like everyone in the stands must have written on her. She had hearts drawn on her face, and her arms and legs looked like she had been to a tattoo parlor. I just shook my head knowing that this was a bittersweet day for Kassie. She had thoroughly enjoyed being around all of her friends for the first time, but I knew she wasn't happy with her performance on the track.

We got home, settled in, changed clothes, and began relaxing. I have to admit I was surprised that Kassie had taken the day's events so well. I headed back to my bedroom to get my watch and rings I had forgotten to put back on after getting cleaned up. As I was sitting on the bed putting them on, Kassie came in. She looked at me and burst into tears.

"Daddy, I'm so sorry I didn't win that race. We all worked so hard, and I didn't come through. I am so sorry!" she sobbed.

I picked her up and held her close, allowing her to weep hard on my shoulder. I told her it was okay, I was so proud of her, and that nobody could have done any better than she had. Feeling her pain of losing for the first time, I put her down and sat back on the bed, looking at her eye to eye.

"How could you be proud of me?" she asked. "I lost! I came in last, Daddy…," and as her voice trailed off into silence, she again quietly muttered, "Last," her head hung in despair.

As I held her small face in my hands, I thought about all the victories that had been accomplished since frantically driving her to the hospital and her emergency air-evac helicopter ride to Phoenix Children's Hospital.

These thoughts reeled through my mind at the speed of light.

- The lack of oxygen to her brain that should have caused irreparable brain damage.
- Her organs shutting down, which should have led to parabolic shutdown.
- The amount of time she fought through the night when there was no hope of survival.
- Hanging in there waiting for the doctor to arrive to try heroic surgery just to give her a chance at survival.
- Surviving ten days on ECMO when no other kid her age had been able to.
- Fighting through the bacterial infection that ravaged her body.
- Living through cutting-edge technology never performed before, allowing her lungs to work separately.
- Fighting off super high fevers that could have killed her.
- Waking up after being in a medically induced coma for two weeks, neurologically intact, and all the while turning the medical profession on its ear.
- Giving hope to people she had never met before as the Miracle Girl on Four.

- Bringing hundreds if not thousands of people together through prayer by not giving up and fighting all the way.
- Gaining enormous respect from professionals who had gotten to know Kassie the kid, not just a patient about to die.
- Teaching herself to walk again and then running in a race one month later.

Even though all of those things and more raced through my head, I didn't hesitate answering her question in less than a heartbeat. We peered into each other's tear-filled eyes as a weary but warm smile began creeping across my face.

"Sweetheart, what are you talking about? Don't you realize, you just won the biggest race of your life. *You're my Longshot to a Miracle!*"

Never Stop, Never Give Up

The following month, when Kassie was scheduled to go back and have her neurological evaluation, she really didn't want to go. She was tired of all the testing and just wanted to get on with her life. I let her know this wasn't a time to have any attitude; the doctor needed to make a true assessment on her behavior, and she needed to act like Kassie.

As we sat there waiting for the doctor, Kassie was messing around with some dinosaur figures that were there in the office. When Dr. Bernes came in, he watched her for a little bit then asked Kassie, "Do you know what those are called?"

Kassie looked at him and responded in true Kassie form, "Um… dinosaurs…DUH!" That was the end of the evaluation.

"I have seen what I needed to see," the doctor said. The rest of Kassie's hour-long appointment was spent by Kassie, and the doctor laughing, joking, and talking about what she planned on doing in the future and how she planned on getting there.

At the end, I asked the doctor about his true opinion of Kassie's situation.

In the doctor's own words, "I would never have expected this in a million years! The amount of time Kassie went without oxygen should not have allowed this result. It truly is a miracle!"

The Christmas after Kassie was released from the hospital, we went back to PCH to visit our friends and to hand out over one hundred of what we called "Kassie Canes" to the kids and their families who were there. Attached to each Kassie Cane was a stuffed animal with the story of what the candy cane represents. She reminded everyone she spoke with to not lose faith and that miracles do happen. Kassie also assured them they were being cared for at the best place in the world, Phoenix Children's Hospital. She showed no fear in sharing that PCH saved her life. We got so much enjoyment out of it ourselves, and the people we spoke with appreciated our visit so much that we decided to make it an annual "father and daughter" event.

Stuffed Tiger with a Christmas
Kassie-cane and story

Long ago there were two villages in a far-off land. One was in a valley, and one was on a mountain top. The people in the mountain village wanted to give each person in the valley a Christmas gift. So the mountain townspeople formed a committee to think of something special. Money was limited, and each gift had to be of equal value to each person. After much time and discussion a decision was finally reached. The town's candy maker, an elderly gentleman who had loved Jesus for many years, came up with an idea—the candy cane. Now, you may be thinking, what is so special about a candy cane—and how can it ever be tied in with the real meaning of Christmas? Well, here is how—and why...

1. **The candy cane is in the shape of a shepherd's staff.** Jesus is our Shepherd, and we are His flock. A sheep follows his own shepherd, knows his voice, trusts him and knows that he is totally safe with him. The sheep will follow no other shepherd than their own. In the same way, if we belong to Jesus, we are to follow only Him. (John 10:11; Psalm 23:1; Isaiah 40:11)

2. **Turned over, the candy cane is a "J,"** the first letter of Jesus' name. (Luke 1:31) It is made of hard candy to remind us that Christ is the "rock" of our salvation.

3. **The wide red stripes on the candy cane represent the blood Jesus shed on the cross** for each one of us so that we can have eternal life through Him. He restores us and cleans us with His shed blood—the only thing that can wash away our sin. (Luke 22:20)

4. **The white stripes on the candy cane represent Jesus' virgin birth and His pure, sinless life.** He is the only human being ever who never committed a single sin, even though He was tempted just as we are. (1 Peter 2:22)

5. **The narrow red stripes on candy canes symbolize Jesus' stripes,** or scars, which He got when He was arrested and whipped. The Bible says we are healed (of sin) because He took those wounds. (Isaiah 53:5; 1 Peter 2:24)

6. **The flavoring in the candy cane is peppermint, which is similar to hyssop.** Hyssop is of the mint family and was used in Old Testament times for purification and sacrifice. (John 19:29; Psalms 51:7)

7. **When we break our candy cane, it reminds us that Jesus' body was broken for us.** When we have communion, it is a reminder of what He did for us. (1 Corinthians 11:24)
8. **AND, if we share our candy cane and give some to someone else because we love that person, we are sharing the love of Jesus.** (1 John 4:7, 8) God gave Himself to us when He sent Jesus to earth to save us. He loves us so much that He wants us to spend eternity with Him. We are assured of that when we accept Jesus into our hearts as our Savior. (John 1:12; John 3:3, 16)

Some people believe this story of the candy cane is only a legend. Others believe it really happened this way. We do not know for sure exactly how the candy cane was invented, but one thing is certain...it is an excellent picture of Christ and His love for you. You can accept Jesus into your heart through a prayer like this:

> Dear God, Thank You for loving me enough to send Jesus for Christmas. I believe Jesus died for my sins, and I accept Him now as my Savior. I promise to follow Him and share His love with others the best that I can. Amen.

After Kassie had been released one year, she had a number of follow-up evaluations scheduled to track her progress. When she was initially released from the hospital, testing had shown that the strep pneumococcal pneumonia had caused Kassie to lose about 25–30 percent of her lung capacity. If she had been a couple years younger, there would have been a chance that her lungs could have improved to allow greater than a 75 percent lung capacity, but that kind of recovery was not likely for a child her age. However, one year later, when Dr. Gong tested her again, she tested out at 100 percent.

Dr. Gong's expression said it all, and in his own words, "I have no medical reason as to why Kassie has this much lung capacity. Her lungs are damaged beyond correction, yet somehow, Kassie's results are nothing short of miraculous."

Kassie continued to work hard at school as well as athletically, and she fought through many challenges along the way. Kassie had the determination of a champion and adopted a "Never Stop, Never Give Up" attitude in everything she did.

Athletically, it took Kassie a few years to get back into true form after teaching herself to walk again when she was eleven. Kassie's entire body needed attention after her illness, and she designed and fanatically adhered to the necessary workout regimen to get her where she wanted to be. Not only did she work on her running technique, but she also worked on her upper and lower body religiously in the weight room and through stretching exercises, and continued that regimen as she got older. I'm not sure she ever regained the gazelle-like grace she enjoyed as a kid, but while she was in high school, she opted to stop playing fast-pitch and for the first time to run track on a team instead. Something I'm sure would have made Coach Cameron from Moon Mountain Elementary School very happy. Kassie received her varsity letters in track, volleyball, and basketball. She set numerous school records in track for the 100-meter, 200-meter, 400-meter, 4×100-meter; then due to a knee injury her sophomore year that kept her from running, Kassie set school records in the field events of shot put, discus, and long jump. She even qualified for State her freshman year in two events.

Kassie received scholarships for volleyball and track, which she used to further her education. One of Kassie's greatest strengths continues to be her compassion for kids. She enjoys giving back, just like everyone did for her when she was recovering. Kassie's long-term goal is to be a coach and motivational speaker. She enjoys being a mentor for kids, helping them to understand you can work through challenges, whatever they may be, to get where you want to be by adopting that "Never Stop, Never Give Up" attitude.

Kassie also still enjoys being a voice, singing praises for Phoenix Children's Hospital, a place not only of medicine, but also one of hope, inspiration, compassion, and enlightenment.

Kassie has been featured in a number of television shows and in print as well. I think Kassie says it best when she says, "Miracles do happen, look at me. I'm here today!"

Kassie's motto—Never Give Up

Never give up-
Life has many Challenges
Give and Receive encouragement
Learn from Life's disappointments
Choose to make your own future
Laugh Daily
143

Kassie

2005 Letter Jacket with
just a few medals

Kassie's senior picture 2005

2005 Track 400 meters—Kassie 1st place—without use of blocks

Track Star—State Bound

Kassie #5 spiking volleyball at Pinnacle H.S.

Kassie #2

Kassie (left) utilizing her 34" Vertical Jump

Stevo, Kassie, Lorrie after PCH Fundraiser

Kassie #7

BIGGER ENEMY

ot only was there some great volleyball played, but the two-day tourna-
it hosted by Peoria Sunrise Mountain High School was for a great cause
lping to raise funds to fight cancer.

ven 4A and 5A ranked teams were among the two dozen entrants in the
. 14 Carol Chase Memorial Volleyball Tournament, played at Sunrise
untain, Glendale Ironwood, and Willow Canyon.

*SportZine
Photos
By
Michael Stevens*

High School Sports—Sportzine Magazine Oct. 2004

A2   © The Arizona Republic   Saturday, May 30, 1998

'Miracle girl' beats survi

— MIRACLE, *from Page A1*

"The one thing I couldn't guarantee was that she would live," he said.

One nurse stayed 36 hours after her shift had ended. Doctors darted in and out of the hospital room, hooking Kassie up to life-support machines. Kassie's parents held her hands, and prayed.

"I told everyone at that hospital, please don't give up on this kid because she won't give up," David Arner said.

Kassie was the fastest runner at Moon Mountain School, her softball team's shortstop who was nicknamed "Speedy," the most ornery of her parents' three children.

"She's a good kid, with a good heart and a good personality, but strong-willed," said her coach, Charlie LeMaster. "That's probably what got her through this."

Kassie credits her friends and family, and her doctors and nurses.

She doesn't remember what they said to her when she slept through the month of March. But they believe she heard them.

They told her she was coaching a team of red blood cells and white blood cells, battling a team of cheating green bacteria cells. They said her team members were as speedy, as skilled and as stubborn as she was. The nursing staff wore red scrubs and the family hung red-and-white jerseys and pompons in the room.

Her 14-year-old sister, Autam, brought her presents each time she was able to boost her oxygen level. Her 9-year-old brother, Steve, kept watch over the tubes that entangled her, and the beeping machines that surrounded her.

Her doctors used a non-traditi[onal] therapy for her infection in whic[h] the blood is pumped out of the body, reoxygenated and pumped back in. Beyda said the survival with that therapy is about 40 per cent.

"But every time we thought '[This] is it,' she'd tell us, 'This isn't it' her own way," Beyda said. "So [she] kept going."

Her parents were there when [Kas]sie opened her eyes in late Marc[h]

The first things she remember[ed] were the stuffed animals piled around her bed, the cards taped [to] the walls and an Elmo backpack [her] family had brought her.

"I thought it was just a big dr[eam] and it was time to wake up," she said. "I saw everybody, but whe[n I] tried to talk to them, I couldn't."

It took almost two weeks unti[l] she could talk. Doctors expected

SATURDAY   5/30/9

INSIDE TODAY

PRAYER

Lord, when we come to a crossroad, not knowing in which direction to go, your loving guidance will lead us on the way you want us to go.

ALMANAC

Today is the 150th day of 1998. . . . In 1431, Joan of Arc, condemned as a heretic, is burned at the stake in Rouen, France. . . . In 1539, Spanish explorer Hernando

KOSOVO ASSURED: Preside[nt] Clinton tells Kosovo's leaders that th[e] United States is consulting with its European partners to ensure an "app[ro]priate, swift and firm response" to e[s]calating Serb attacks on their homel[and]. **A28**

l odds

emain in the hospital three
iths. But Kassie rebounded
:kly, leaving after five weeks, in
e to enter her school's track and
d competition she'd won the year
ıre.

'or the first time, she came in

I was just glad to be there," she
.

ince the meet, she has shaved
seconds off her time in the 50-
l dash. But she doesn't dwell on
progress of the past few weeks.
assie doesn't talk much either
ıt the hearing aids she now must
г, though her hearing has im-
red to about a 50 percent loss
ı 90 percent. When she men-
s the weeks she can't remember,
s slip from her eyes.
It changed my life, with my
ties, with my hearing," Kassie
, wiping away a tear. "I couldn't
my own voice at first."
he would rather talk about her
cockatiel "Sunny," or the soda
hine her family won, or her
ıall team. The smiles come easi-
ıat way.
Vhen Kassie began physical re-
litation last month, she couldn't
ı 2-pound weight using both
ıs.
ow, she can curl almost 60
ıds.
ill, her softball coach said he
г expected to see her back. But
ıesday, she joined her team for
ıst game of the season. She

Michael Chow/The Arizona Republic

Her ordeal "changed my life," says Kassie Arner, who is continuing to recoup at home with her mother, Lorrie, and her brother, Steve.

scored a run that helped her team advance to the championships.

Her teammates are back to calling her "Speedy." But her father has a new nickname: "Long Shot."

"I never have to worry ever again about whether there is a God or not," he said. "I've witnessed miracle after miracle."

Jennifer Barrett can be reached at 444-7113 or jennifer.barrett@pni.com via e-mail.

Family Christmas at the new home

It's close to midnight, and Dave Arner is all smiles as he strides onto the Critical Care Unit at Phoenix Children's Hospital, bearing pies for the night shift employees. He has paid other visits during daytime hours, but it seems important to include every shift in his ongoing expression of gratitude.

"Anything we can do for PCH — that's how we feel," he said.

Emotions still run deep as he remembers the night last March when Critical Care staff gave his daughter Kassie a 5 percent chance of living.

It seemed impossible. Eleven-year-old Kassie, gregarious and athletic, had always managed to stay well when other family members became ill. But she'd become run down while juggling practices and games for both softball and basketball, eventually coming down with the flu. One afternoon she took a nap on the couch and never woke up.

By the time she arrived at PCH, a lung had filled with fluid and her organs had begun to shut down. Tests showed severe oxygen deprivation. Doctors diagnosed strep pneumonia, and told the Arners their daughter probably would not make it through the night.

Dave, desperate to do something besides wait, went to each staff member personally and said, "Don't give up on this kid. This kid's got a lot of fight in her. She knows what it's like to be down and come back to win."

Kassie proved her dad's statement by surviving the night — which Dave calls "the first miracle." Still, she remained in grave danger. Doctors decided to place her on ECMO, a heart-lung bypass machine that is used only when all other treatments have failed.

The equipment would be attached through an opening in the neck, and staff gave Kassie a 50 percent chance of surviving the required surgery. Dave and his wife, Lorrie, were optimistic, in light of the grim odds that had been presented to them the night before.

"I've never been so happy to have a 50/50 chance in my life," Dave said.

By then Kassie's case was drawing a good deal of attention. Prayer lines extended from Hawaii to Florida, and Kassie's room was quickly filling up with cards and stuffed animals. PCH staff gave up trying to keep a safe emotional detachment from the girl.

"They were literally trading shifts so they could stay with Kassie," Dave said.

When the Arners learned that the surgery had been successful, Dave called Kassie's 9-year-old brother, Steve, to tell him the news. In Steve's mind, the 50/50 odds his sister had been given were reason enough to celebrate. "She went from a 5 percent chance to a 50 percent chance!" he said. "That's great!"

But there remained quite a battle ahead. Kassie was still unconscious, and her oxygen level remained dangerously low — about 40 percent of the normal level. Dave, with his brother's help, invented a game to tap his daughter's competitive streak. He told her she

was coaching Team Red and White, made up of blood and oxygen that needed to travel throughout her body. Her players were smart and fast, he explained, but they were pitted against a nasty team of players that cheated constantly.

Kassie's 14-year-old sister, Autam, began a game of her own: each time Kassie showed progress, she would receive a small reward — candy, a bottle of fingernail polish or a pair of colorful socks.

Kassie's progress fluctuated, and Dave remembers four or five times they almost lost her. "Every day that she survived was a milestone," he said. As she began to regain consciousness, the Arners had to face the fear that Kassie's oxygen deprivation might have resulted in brain damage. She couldn't speak at first, but Dave remembers the moment she made deliberate eye contact with him. "I could tell that she knew who I was," he said. "That was the first I knew she was in there."

She moved to the Subacute Unit, where physical therapists worked to strengthen her weakened muscles. Kassie knew she would be allowed to go home when she had regained the ability to perform ordinary tasks such as dressing herself and walking without help. Recovery was expected to take several months. Three weeks later, when she jogged down the unit's hallway, doctors decided it was time to send her home.

"They said it was more than they could have asked for," Dave said. She was discharged from the hospital the next day.

Three weeks later her school held its annual Field Day, where Kassie had won most of the events the previous year. Determined to participate, she competed in the 50-yard-dash — and came in last. She approached her dad with tears in her eyes, telling him, "I lost."

Dave could only smile as he tried to put the matter into perspective.

"Sweetheart, you don't understand," he said. "You just had the biggest win of your life."

Story Sponsored By

SheaHomes
The Confidence Builder

VOL. 4B   THE NEWSLETTER OF CARING & SHARING FROM PHOENIX CHILDREN'S HOSPITAL   SUMMER 1999

Kassie: The Biggest Win

It's close to midnight, and Dave Arner is all smiles as he strides onto the Critical Care Unit at Phoenix Children's Hospital, bearing pies for the night shift employees. He has paid other visits during daytime hours, but it seems important to include every shift in his ongoing expression of gratitude.

"Anything we can do for PCH — that's how we feel," he said.

Emotions still run deep as he remembers the night last year when Critical Care staff gave his daughter Kassie a 5 percent chance of living.

It seemed impossible. Eleven-year-old Kassie, gregarious and athletic, had always managed to stay well when other family members became ill. But she'd become run down while juggling practices and games for both softball and basketball, eventually coming down with the flu. One afternoon she took a nap on the couch and never woke up.

By the time she arrived at PCH, a lung had filled with fluid and her organs had begun to shut down. Tests showed severe oxygen deprivation. Doctors diagnosed strep pneumonia, and told the Arners their daughter probably would not make it through the night.

Dave, desperate to do something besides wait, went to each staff member personally and said, "Don't give up on this kid. This kid's got a lot of fight in her. She knows what it's like to be down and come back to win."

Kassie proved her dad's statement by surviving the night — which Dave calls "the first miracle." Still, she remained in grave danger. Doctors decided to place her on ECMO, a heart-lung bypass machine that is used only when all other treatments have failed.

The equipment would be attached through an opening in the neck, and staff gave Kassie a 50 percent chance of surviving the required surgery. Dave and his wife, Lorrie, were optimistic, in light of the grim odds

that had been presented to them the night before.

"I've never been so happy to have a 50/50 chance in my life," Dave said.

By then Kassie's case was drawing a good deal of attention. Prayer lines extended from Hawaii to Florida, and Kassie's room was quickly filling up with cards and stuffed animals. PCH staff gave up trying to keep a safe emotional detachment from the girl.

"They were literally trading shifts so they could stay with Kassie," Dave said.

When the Arners learned that the surgery had been successful, Dave called Kassie's 9-year-old brother, Steve, to tell him the news. In Steve's mind the 50/50 odds his sister had been given were reason enough to celebrate. "She went from a 5 percent chance to a 50 percent chance!" he said. "That's great!"

But there remained quite a battle ahead. Kassie was still unconscious, and her oxygen level remained dangerously low — about 40 percent of the normal level. Dave, with his brother's help, invented a game to tap his daughter's competitive streak. He told her she was coaching Team Red and White, made up of blood and oxygen that needed to travel throughout her body. Her players were smart and fast, he explained, but they were pitted against a nasty team of players that cheated constantly.

Kassie's 14-year-old sister, Autam, began a game of her own: each time Kassie showed progress, she would receive a small reward — candy, a bottle of fingernail polish or a pair of colorful socks.

Kassie's progress fluctuated, and Dave remembers four or five times they almost lost her. "Every day that she survived was a milestone," he said. As she began to regain consciousness, the Arners had to face the fear that Kassie's oxygen deprivation might have resulted in brain damage. She couldn't speak at first, but Dave remembers the moment she made deliberate eye contact with him. "I could tell that she knew who I was," he said. "That was the first I knew she was in there."

She moved to the Subacute Unit, where physical therapists worked to strengthen her weakened muscles. Kassie knew she would be allowed to go home when she had regained the ability to perform ordinary tasks such as dressing herself and walking without help. Recovery was expected to take several months. Three weeks later, when she jogged down the unit's hallway, doctors decided it was time to send her home.

"They said it was more than they could have asked for," Dave said. She was discharged from the hospital the next day.

Three weeks later her school held its annual Field Day, where Kassie had won most of the events the previous year. Determined to participate, she competed in the 50-yard dash — and came in last. She approached her dad with tears in her eyes, telling him, "I lost."

Dave could only smile as he tried to put the matter into perspective.

"Sweetheart, you don't understand," he said. "You just had the biggest win of your life."

Miracles happen!

Shadows lurked in the hospital room as Lorrie Arner held her 11-year-old daughter's limp hand. This is no place for you, Kassie, she thought. You should be outside hitting homers!

Suddenly, terror seized the Phoenix mom: any moment could be her little girl's last. How am I supposed to say goodbye to you? she sobbed.

Just days earlier, Kassie had returned from softball practice sluggish and coughing.

"She's amazing," says Lorrie of Kassie, second from left, with her family.

Kassie's comeback

Most moms know what it's like to have a battle of wills with a stubborn child—and Lorrie Arner's daughter was as headstrong as they come. But that may be what saved her—that and a whole lot of love

"Looks like the flu," Lorrie sighed, phoning the pediatrician.

But over the next few days, Kassie felt so crummy that all she did was sleep.

"Mom," Autam, 14, frowned. "Kassie's breathing funny."

Lorrie tried to wake her, but she wouldn't budge. Panicked, her husband David called the doctor, who said, "Get her to the hospital immediately!"

By the time they reached Phoenix Children's Hospital, Kassie's lips and fingertips were blue. As

"Our Kassie's a fighter," David pleaded. "Please don't give up on her"

physicians hooked her up to a respirator, Lorrie cried, "Why won't she wake up?"

A specialist soon discovered why. "Your daughter's lungs are inflamed with strep pneumoniae," he said. "It's a bacteria that usually causes ear infections. But because Kassie's lungs were weakened by the flu, her lungs are devastated. Her oxygen level is only forty percent of what it should be."

"There must be something you can do!" David pleaded.

"We'll keep her sedated and treat her with antibiotics," the doctor explained. "But there's only a five-percent chance Kassie will live through the night."

As the sky grew dark, Lorrie was filled with despair. How did things go so wrong so quickly? she anguished.

But David's eyes sparked with

hope. "They don't know how headstrong our girl is," he said.

Lorrie nodded. Her little tomboy was strong-willed, all right. "You're not the boss of me!" she'd announced at three, tiny arms folded across her chest. And when she was learning to ride her two-wheeler, she'd scowl each time she tipped over, then climb right back on again.

"It's true," Lorrie agreed. "If anyone can fight this, it's Kassie."

That night, nearly 40 loved ones crowded into Kassie's room to pray. "Our Kassie's a fighter," David told her doctors. "Please, don't give up on her."

"Well," Robin Laks, M.D., said. "My shift just ended, but I'll stick around to fight with Kassie." Then she joined hands with the group and prayed.

And as the sun rose, there was good news. "Kassie is continuing to fight," Dr. Laks explained. "But with her lungs not pumping enough oxygen, her heart could stop beating."

But there was a last resort: a heart-lung machine called an ECMO that would cleanse Kassie's blood of bacteria, add oxygen and then recirculate it through her body.

"It's a long shot," doctors cautioned. "It's usually reserved for newborns. We've never tried it on a child Kassie's age."

"She's *our* baby," Lorrie murmured. And now, as she sat at Kassie's bedside, she prayed, Lord, no one expected my little girl to live through the night. You sent us

one miracle . . . grant us another!

Within hours, Kassie's blood oxygen level rose to 50 percent. And over the next few days, as she lay in a coma, visitors continued to hold vigil.

Knowing what an athlete Kassie was, her Uncle Steve said, "Think of yourself as the coach of a team of red and white blood cells against a team of green bacteria. Now get out there and fight those nasty bacteria and win the game!"

Later, Kassie's classmates came by. "Everyone wants you to make a speedy recovery, Speedy!" Lorrie cried, using the nickname Kassie's friends had given her as they plastered their softball jerseys and red-and-white balloons on the wall. And the following morning, nurse Arva Bynum arrived wearing crimson scrubs.

"I want to be on Kassie's team too," she said.

Although Kassie remained motionless, her vital signs were improving. And when her oxygen levels rose to 60 percent, Autam brought her nail polish.

"I'll give you a manicure when you get well," she whispered.

When Kassie's levels passed 70,

Autam fastened a bracelet around her sister's wrist to celebrate.

"I think the only reason she's alive is because she's such an athlete," doctors marveled.

"That, and the fact that she has a stubborn streak a mile long," Lorrie sighed. But inside, she was paralyzed with fear. What if the fight was too hard?

Yet after eight days in the hospital, Kassie was so strong, she was removed from the ECMO. And a few mornings later, she woke up. "I want to go home," she announced. "Like, *now*."

Lorrie burst into tears of relief. "Oh, Kassie," she breathed. "You're as ornery as ever!"

But in the hallway, the doctors' expressions were somber. "Kassie isn't out of the woods yet," they warned. "It'll take her at least three months to recover, and her lungs may never be the same."

Yet Kassie set out to prove them wrong—again. Although she could barely hold a two-pound weight, she flung herself into rehabilitation—and was soon lifting nearly 60 pounds! In fact, after a month, she was sprinting down the corridor to the therapy room, taunting her doctor. "Wanna race?"

"Okay," he grinned. "You can go home tomorrow!"

That night, Lorrie beamed as she helped Kassie stuff her getwell gifts into her Elmo back-

"Kassie's not out of the woods just yet," doctors warned

pack (the cool thing among the pre-teen crowd.)

Ten days later, Kassie—whose lungs were at 80 percent capacity—was back at school running the 50-yard dash on Field Day. Although she was the last to cross the finish line, David and Lorrie couldn't have been prouder.

And the next week, Kassie was playing shortstop again, batting in the winning run that took her team to the championships.

Today, Kassie's a spirited and healthy sixth-grader.

"I used to think her stubbornness was a character flaw," Lorrie says. "But now I know it was a blessing in disguise."

—**Heather Black**

WHEN TO WORRY ABOUT THE FLU

While the flu can leave a person susceptible to infections that can lead to pneumonia and heart or kidney problems, Marc Russert, M.D., says what happened to Kassie is rare.

Symptoms of a normal flu are fatigue, muscle aches, a sore throat and fever. Call your doctor if the fever lasts more than 72 hours or the cough, pain or chest discomfort becomes severe.

The best way to protect yourself is to get a flu vaccination each October," Dr. Russert advises. Even kids can get them; contact your pediatrician to find out more.

10/6/98 *WOMAN'S WORLD* 35

Woman's World article—Oct 6, 1998

From Kassie

W hen I was eleven years old, I was a child looking forward to entering my teen years. I began to want to know "who I was and what my purpose was." I began to understand and question right from wrong on a bigger scale than just what we know as being a kid. I was at the beginning of developing my own set of beliefs and morals.

Being an eleven-year-old, I was making decisions, looking into different forms of spirituality whether I believe in some sort of higher power or science. Belief and belonging is something I struggled with from a young age.

I was raised Baptist and loved going to church with my family and grandparents. I enjoyed singing within the community and being surrounded with love and affection from one another.

After I got sick, it was hard for me to understand why God would make me go through what I went through, and why God made my wonderful parents and siblings have to watch from the sidelines and feel hopeless and completely helpless.

I need to state with no uncertain terms, I do believe in a higher power, and He works in our lives daily. I fought with myself all the way through adulthood whether it was the power of prayer or if it was science that is what kept me alive. I believe now it was a combination of both, working with each other in tandem. I know those who were witness to my illness and the miracles that occurred don't have this struggle that I did, because they saw it with their own eyes. But I had a hard time accepting that God only puts things in front of you that will challenge what you are capable of and make you stronger.

At the age of eleven, I was a girl who lived life to the fullest. I was popular and friends with everyone. I felt bigger than life! I was the fastest girl in school and could even outrun the boys. I had a certain charm about me and was confident with who I was. I was never the one who got sick, while other family members did.

I was engaged with track and field, I played competitive softball, I was a cheerleader; yet I enjoyed throwing the football around with Stevo's football team. I was up for anything put in front of me, whether I knew how to play the sport or not, it came natural and easy.

When I got sick, my life got put on hold...or should I say, it completely stopped. Because of my state of health, I don't remember what happened, but I know what I am saying is the truth. My lungs failed me, and my breathing became shallow. When I got to the first hospital closest to my house, they could tell my only chance of survival was to be air-evac'd by helicopter to Phoenix Children's Hospital. Even then, once I arrived, it was determined I had a slim chance at best for survival. My ONLY chance was to be put in a medically induced coma and placed on ten days of ECMO, an extremely heroic effort by the doctors of PCH. They were willing to do this because they saw I was a fighter, actually surviving the night, when medically I shouldn't have.

When I came out of the coma, none of this made sense to me. I was a very healthy and strong athletic girl. Why and how could something like this even take place? When I woke up, I was broken. I had my body, such that it was, but I wasn't able to do anything but lie there. I couldn't make anything work. I was so scared. I wasn't able to read, write, walk, and talk. I was completely oblivious as to who I now was as a person. My mirrors were covered so I couldn't see myself because I looked nothing like me anymore. I had no idea that I had become nearly deaf. I was completely lost and unsure where I was or what I was even supposed to do. I didn't understand why I had so many machines hooked up to my body, let alone why I was surrounded by strangers, who later I was to find out were my family members. Talk about a whirlwind of emotionless emotion as I laid there not able to move. It's like I went to sleep after Mom gave me some medicine, and I woke up to all of this. I was mentally unable to grasp the concept of what I had gone through.

After a few days, my memory started to come back to me, and I began to remember who people were.

I remember the power of prayer and how many people spoke of the white light that was sheltering me and helping me to become stronger. I eventually was able to gain some weight and began my journey of physical therapy. Coming from a girl who had won every race I had ever entered, I was confident this was going to be a piece of cake. Boy was I wrong. I couldn't support myself standing up. Heck, I had to have help just to be able to sit up straight without falling over.

My parents, family, friends, and doctors were my number one cheerleaders and kept telling me I could do this. I just had to trick my brain into being confident that I had beaten strep pneumo. Now I needed to fight for this next stage, and it was going to be even harder than the first.

My dad had a way of making things that were confusing to me, make sense. He helped me understand that this next challenge was the only way to get back up and running and racing. I had the heart and desire of a true athlete. I didn't understand a lot of things, but I was determined to walk again. I remember I had a walker to help me walk around the circle, which was pretty tiny. It's where the doctors sat and watched over us. Something you could completely and easily walk around in about ten seconds. Yet it took me about twenty-five minutes to even get halfway with all the baby steps and breather breaks I needed to take. I was swarmed with emotions and cried a lot asking why I couldn't do it. This was something that was once so simple to me, and I couldn't even put one foot in front of the other now. My lungs always felt like they were going to explode, and I got lightheaded very easily. I eventually got the encouragement and trust within myself that if I really wanted to get out of the hospital, I had to fight hard and get through my tears. Nobody could do it for me. It had to come from me, myself, and I.

As a preteen, I believed I once had all the skills to take on the world. I was raised extremely independent, for it was a great and essential skill both my parents raised me on. My mom always pushed me to become the best person I was capable of being. She was who took all of us kids to our sporting events and made sure she was at nearly every single one. Having three kids, that's not easy. I say I have my dad's big heart and my mom's bullheadedness, which later in life I came to find out was a blessing in disguise. Thank God, I'm ornery, or I wouldn't be here to tell you this now.

After I got out of the hospital, real life became real. I had to work for everything I got. I'm not just talking about physically becoming an athlete again, I'm talking every aspect of my life. School was no longer easy. I couldn't hear the teachers. They had to change how they did their jobs to accommodate me in the classroom. I needed to read their lips. I had to have someone take notes for me because I couldn't write, read lips, and try to understand what was going on all at the same time. It was a nightmare. I went from being a B student to Cs if I worked really hard, did extra homework, and went to tutors and the evening learning centers. Ds and Fs now became part of my life. It was demoralizing and disheartening to work so hard and not to achieve the goal you set out to hit.

When high school came along, it was even more challenging. Although I had all the documentation to back up my disability, some teachers automatically thought I was slacking because I was an athlete, and that I just needed to apply myself more. In reality, I was putting in more time studying, doing homework, and spending time with special tutors than either Autam or Stevo was, and they were sailing through school. It was hard for me to understand why that was, were they just smarter than me? Mom and Dad continually told me that wasn't the case, and circumstances were very different, but it still hurt. It was offered that maybe I should go into the special ed classes and make it easier for myself, but I didn't want that for myself and neither did Mom and Dad. Dad raised us to never be a victim, and I did my very best to never act like I was.

There was a "no pass, no play" rule in our school district so that heaped even more pressure on me to do well. I was told by some teachers that college just wasn't in my future, and that's okay. That upset me and made me even more determined to get through high school.

When I graduated high school, I received a double scholarship for track and volleyball. I represented Team USA for indoor volleyball and traveled to Australia and Hawaii, even had my own rooting section from the local boys, imagine that… LOL. I received my associate's degree and went to school for kinesiology and teaching.

I have managed and became a director for Beginners Edge Sports Training in Scottsdale, Arizona. I have worked for BEST in Arizona and California since 2010 and coach eighteen-month-olds all the way up to twelve-year-olds, as well as private sessions for the older teenagers. I coach everything and take after my dad coaching both girls and boys sports. I would still like to be a motivational speaker someday, telling my story and raising money for children's hospitals nationwide.

I have also been a teacher at a private school for younger children's education as well as special needs. I nannied for over fifteen years with multiple families whom I am still in contact with, and their little ones are now in college… wow!

We thought because of all the radiation I had, I probably wouldn't be able to get pregnant or carry a pregnancy to full term. In honesty, I've had my share of miscarriages, but I have been blessed with two little boys, Khaison was born in 2014 and Maverick in 2020.

I have witnessed much joy and much heartache. My life hasn't always been an easy one. I have dealt with many ups and downs and emotional scars because of my hearing. I have endured many physical setbacks due to my illness, but I have fought through everything even though I was hospitalized a few times doing so. I am a fighter for my family, and even today I refuse to buckle. No matter what the odds are, Never Stop, Never Give Up!

My symbol represents my life challenges that I've overcome, and my "Never Stop, Never Give Up" philosophy.

The Feather represents Elegance and Beauty, Inside and Out.

The Spiral is to Engage My Core's Inner Strength, "Spirit Chakra".

The Loop de Loops are to help Guide Me and keep me Inside the Correct Lanes.

The Two Daggers are to represent my Early Childhood Illness… as well as something Traumatic that happened to me in my teenage years.

The Two Small Circles represent the many Curveball / Obstacles that have been Thrown in my Direction.

The Arrowhead has an Extended Point, Extremely Sharp, able to Pierce Through Anything that is put in front of me.

I will always "Find It" inside me the desire to continue to Grow and become the BEST Version of Myself.

My dad helped me to understand our lives are on a one-way path, picture a 5-lane road.

The middle lane is the safest, not much can happen to you there, but it tends to be a bit boring. It's pretty slow moving.

The next two lanes on each side are still safe, but you need to watch for challenges that can pop out towards you at times. Not as boring for sure and things happen a bit faster.

The two outside lanes are ok in small doses, not necessarily always safe, but also not full of too much danger. There can be a lot more challenges and they can pop into your lane at any time without much warning, if any. Much Much Faster.

Outside the 5 lanes in the Rough, is Havoc and Danger. You can lose yourself, and even your life if you stay outside in the Rough too much. Things happen too FAST and with no warning because you have no time to watch out for them; you're always dodging and changing course. In the Rough, you have No Control of yourself or your surroundings. Extremely Fast Moving.

As you can see, I have had many twists and turns. My life hasn't always been easy and I still struggle, but I have always had a direction. I get into those outside lanes occasionally and have even wandered into the Rough at times, but my "Never Stop, Never Give Up" philosophy has always helped direct me back to the middle 3 lanes where my Life, Family, and Love of Life reside.

Khaison and Maverick 2020

Kassie, Khaison, and Maverick Arner

I get a gift, a handmade book of Longshot to a Miracle from my
family. Stevo and Sarah, Autam, and Kassie.
Not pictured, Eamonn and Lorrie.

David E. Arner is married and the father of three children, two
daughters and a son. Dave sees the best in people and aspires to help
others reach their own positive outcomes. He was born in Seminole,
Oklahoma, where he learned from his parents, siblings, grandparents, aunts, and uncles that family is the most important thing in life.
He's upbeat and positive, gregarious, and outgoing. He has focused
his life around building and strengthening the foundations of his
coworkers and community…and plans to have as much FUN as possible while he's at it! He exudes integrity, is kind, generous, and is
very considerate of family, friends, and others. His warm and sincere
smile puts you at ease immediately.

Dave has many interests. In his younger years, he was a lead singer in a rock band, he raced cars on the quarter mile track, and he managed restaurants. Currently, he mentors young adults, sings, and enjoys a successful Real Estate career. He is a great communicator and speaks easily to most everyone.

Other than his family, perhaps what Dave is most proud of is his coaching of young athletes ranging in age from seven to eighteen for over thirty years. Partnering with parents on how to best help their athlete to grow and prosper. Directly working with the boys and girls in multiple sports, helping them to get to the next level; whatever that may be for them.

It warms Dave's heart when these athletes—grown up and sometimes unrecognizable to him—call him coach. He says, "It's great! I'll be at a grocery store or someplace, and I'll hear someone yell out COACH!" It's truly humbling when they state they had fun and learned a lot while they were on his team, not just about the sport but about how to deal and cope with unforeseen challenges. Dave says, "Sports can be a stepping stone for some athletes toward higher education and can teach kids how to think on the fly, enhancing outcomes. That is a very good trait to have in life."

Even before Dave had children of his own, he coached, because he believes that organized team sports promote "synergy," showing kids from an early age the benefits of working together for a greater outcome than they could achieve by themselves. Dave promotes applying a strong work ethic early will allow you to go much further, whether it's in sports, school, or a profession. Life happens, and you need to be ready.

The story of *Longshot to a Miracle* culminated everything that Dave learned throughout his life into a precise moment in time, where life and death literally hung in the balance.

CPSIA information can be obtained
at www.ICGtesting.com
Printed in the USA
LVHW070149271121
704402LV00004B/8